CW00515712

MIAMI

Part of the Langenscheidt Publishing Group

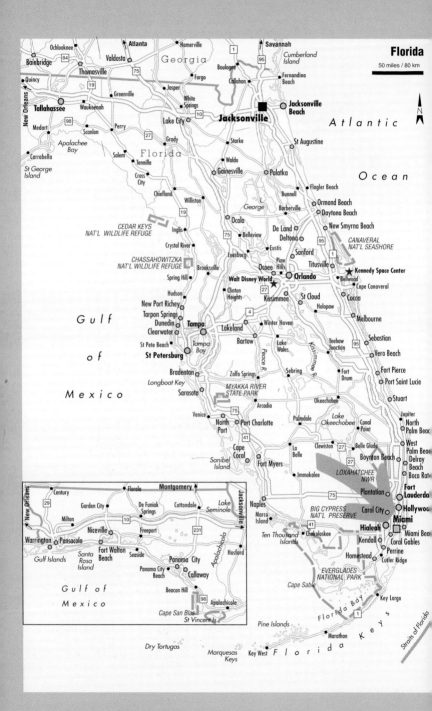

Welcome!

This guidebook combines the interests and enthusiasms of two of the world's best-known information providers: Insight Guides, who have set the standard for visual travel guides since 1970, and Discovery Channel, the world's premier source of nonfiction television programming.

Its aim is to help visitors get the most out of this dynamic city during a short stay, and to this end Insight's correspondent in Florida, Joann Biondi, has devised a series of itineraries linking the essential sights. The guide begins with three full-day itineraries exploring Miami's most popular areas (downtown Miami and Bayside Marketplace; the historic Art Deco district of South Miami Beach; and the whimsical neighborhood of Coconut Grove), followed by seven half-day itineraries exploring other interesting areas and aspects of the city, such as a Cuban cigar factory in Little Havana, the exotic neighborhood of Little Haiti, a coral rock lagoon in Coral Gables, a Renaissance-style palace, and sun-soaked Windsurfer Beach. In addition to the city itineraries there are two excursions: one to the wetlands of Everglades National Park and the other to Key Largo.

Supporting the itineraries are sections on history and culture, shopping, eating out and nightlife, plus a a calendar of events, and a fact-packed practical information section that includes tips on getting there, getting around, etc, as well as ideas on where to stay.

Joann Biondi is a freelance writer and college professor who has also been the project editor of *Insight Guide: Miami* and a major contributor to other Florida-based Insight titles. Having lived in the city since the 1970s in a series of wild and wonderful houses, Biondi's intimate knowledge ensures she is the perfect host for your stay in South Florida.

C O N T E N T S

Pages 2/3:
fantastic
Florida sunset

Excursions

Two fascinating, and very different, Florida experiences far away from the city

Pages 8/9: mirror images in Miami

Shopping, Eating Out & Nightlife

Calendar of Events

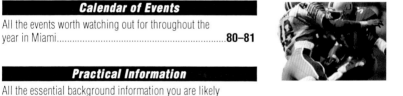

Practical Information

Maps

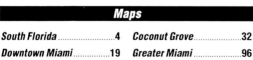

HISTORY

Early Years

Miami is a vibrant, ethnically rich sun-belt baby of a city that greets newcomers with open arms. Its lifestyle is informal and its people gregarious. Music, dance and warm-weather good times are taken for granted. How it came to be this way is not a long story. In the beginning there were Indians. Seminole tribes inhabited the dense, virgin South Florida landscape for centuries before European explorers landed on its shores. Their lives were simple and in harmony with nature. They worked with tools made from seashells and hunted the abundant wild game found in the environs.

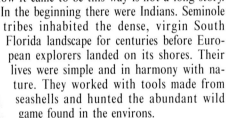

Native Florida Indian

All that changed when Juan Ponce de Leon, the Spaniard who traveled the world in search of the fountain of youth, sailed into Biscayne Bay in 1513. And, as in most stories of covetous white explorers, his arrival was followed by a series of violent encounters. For the next 50 years, the Spaniards tried to 'conquer' the land and the Indians they found. Both were a challenge. Then came the French and British who were also interested in Florida's prospects. In 1763, the French and Indian War ended with Florida a British colony. But shortly after that, in 1784, Britain decided to swap with Spain and traded Florida for the nearby Bahama Islands.

By the 1800s, Florida was a haven for run-away slaves fleeing the South and in 1821, the US gained control of the peninsula.

Americans began claiming land along the banks of the Miami River. From 1835 to 1857, a series of Indian attacks occurred of which the most noted was the Dade Massacre in which Major Francis L Dade (after whom the county is named) was killed. During the 1860s and 70s, the first of the northern developers, whose names are now immortalized in local street signs, began to claim their stake in Miami.

William B Brickell from Ohio bought land on the Miami River. Ralph M Munroe of New York's Staten Island settled into what would become Coconut Grove. Bahamians, with their tropical know-how, were brought over to help build the city. Flora McFarlane worked to establish the first library.

Julia Tuttle, daughter of early settler Ephraim T Sturtevant, played a pivotal

Julia Sturtevant Tuttle

role in Miami's development. She convinced Henry M Flagler to extend his railroad from Palm Beach to Miami. In the cold winter of 1894–5, when Palm Beach was beset by frost, Tuttle sent Flagler a bouquet of Miami orange blossoms that had survived the cold. Flagler, tempted by Miami's warm possibilities, rolled his train into town in 1896, and that same year Miami officially became a city.

The Boom-Time 1900s
In the early 1900s there was a modest growth boom for the area. Government Cut, which later became the Port of Miami, was dredged; Miami Beach became a city and began sprouting holiday hotels; and America's rich – like James Deering who built the Renaissance-style palace of Vizcaya – started to build lavish homes on waterfront properties.

The brutal hurricane of 1926

The Roaring Twenties brought a rush of land developers who carved out communities like the Mediterranean-inspired Coral Gables, and the University of Miami became a reality. But the 1920s also brought one of the most brutal hurricanes ever to hit the city. Boats were grounded, buildings demolished, and over 100 people were killed in the 1926 storm. Another monster hurricane would follow in 1935. But Miami bounced back and in the 1930s the city again flourished. This was the era of the great Art Deco hotels that would make the southern end of Miami Beach world famous. Over 500 of the futuristic structures were built – all with the Deco details of racing stripes, geometric patterns, neon lights, and playful pastel colors. Tourists flocked to the faddish, eye-candy hotels and danced to the big band sounds that filled the ocean-side streets.

During World War II, many of those flamingo-pink hotels were transformed into hospitals and barracks for the thousands of US soldiers who were stationed in Miami for military training. In the waters off the coast, German submarines roamed the deep. When the war ended the mood lifted and Miami Beach returned to being America's playground, and a home-base for many of the country's most notorious mobsters who grew rich on illegal gambling.

Fidel Castro

Elderly Jews, fleeing the bitter cold winters of the Northeast, also settled in the area.

The 1950s brought more tourism growth to Miami. This time the hotels being built in the middle of Miami Beach were luxurious and grand with crystal chandeliers and marble floors. The Fontainebleau and Eden Roc Hotels became known for their pleasure-packed vacations catering to an elite class of tourists. Air-conditioning became a necessity rather than a luxury, and the area's population hit 1 million.

Enter Fidel

The tail end of the 1950s, however, brought a drastic change to Miami. In the nearby Caribbean island of Cuba, a brazen revolutionary with a

12

Old postcard of Miami Beach

flowing black beard seized control of the country in 1959. He was to have as much impact on life in Miami as he had on Havana.

President Fidel Castro, declaring himself a socialist, sent shock waves through the Western hemisphere. His confiscating of property and nationalizing of island businesses caused many of Cuba's most affluent citizens to flee the country and Miami, with its similar climate and close proximity, seemed a natural destination for the refugees. In the years that followed, hundreds of thousands of Cubans seeking political asylum boarded 'freedom flights' to Miami, thus planting the seed that would eventually transform Miami from a small American city most noted for its sun and fun mentality into a bustling, cosmopolitan metropolis often called the capital of Latin America.

The first wave of Cuban refugees

A CIA-organized attempt to overthrow Castro and take over the island – the Bay of Pigs invasion – failed in 1961. It was followed by the 1962 Cuban Missile Crisis which created the threat of war with Soviet-supported Cuba. The tense confrontation ended when President John F Kennedy promised that the US would not again try to invade Cuba. Miami's Cuban exile community now had to face the fact that they were not likely to be going home and that any hope of a family reunion meant that their relatives would have to join them in Miami.

Throughout the 1960s, Cuban exiles settled into the once-Anglo neighborhood west of downtown Miami and began calling it Little Havana. Eventually, their presence spread to all parts of the city. Since many of the so-called first wave of Cuban immigrants were

Easter Mass in Little Haiti

members of the professional and entrepreneurial class, many brought with them valuable skills and remnants of past family wealth that enabled them to set up professions and small businesses – Cuban cafeterias, coffee shops and cigar factories – to cater to the exile clientele.

It was this first wave of energetic Cubans that helped to make Miami a predominantly Hispanic city that would in time draw thousands more immigrants from throughout Central and South America. The latter came because of the lack of opportunities in their own countries, and the ease with which they could settle into the local community and find a job without having the need to speak English.

Paradise Lost

The 1970s started out on a positive note for Miami. The Miami Dolphins football team brought winning-streak pride to the city, President Richard M Nixon vacationed on Key Biscayne, and the Cuban community seemed to be assimilating to life in the US. But the economic recession that plagued the country also created hard times for Miami. Unemployment rose to 13 percent, major downtown construction projects were abandoned, and Miami's international banking community hit financial problems.

Haitian immigrants started sailing to Miami in rickety wooden boats in search of a better life. Their plight – escaping the severe poverty and iron-fisted dictatorship of their Caribbean homeland – was understandable to the Miami community, but since they were not fleeing a Communist country, their entry into the US was not as warmly welcomed by the authorities as was that of the Cubans.

Miami's African-American community felt the crunch of economic woes the hardest. Already down-trodden and poor, many lost out on jobs that were taken by recent Cuban immigrants, and with Spanish on its way to becoming a necessity for employment, blacks became even more marginalized by the system.

Mariel refugees sailing to Miami

The year 1980 is remembered as one of Miami's most turbulent. A white police officer charged with the slaying of a black insurance salesman was acquitted. The city's black community was outraged and the largely black neighborhood of Liberty City erupted in violence. The riots ended with 18 people dead and damage to property totaling $100 million.

Later that year, President Fidel Castro allowed 125,000 Cubans to leave the island in a massive boat-lift from the Cuban port of Mariel. Miami Cubans were jubilant at being re-united with relatives, but the US government later learned that many of those *Marielitos* were actually convicted criminals and patients of mental hospitals that Castro wanted to get rid of.

Also that year, the body of the former president of Nicaragua, Anastasio Somoza, was buried in a Little Havana cemetery. Many Nicaraguan refugees fleeing Communist rule moved to Miami. The mood in Miami during the early 1980s was bleak. Anglos started leaving the area in search of a more 'American' environment. Bumper stickers stating "Will the last American leaving Miami please bring the flag" became commonplace across the country.

Bahamian street musicians in Coconut Grove

Cocaine cowboys infiltrated the city. The drug-smuggling industry was said to be pumping over $10 billion a year into the local economy. Real estate brokers didn't blink at the boxes of cash that were often used to buy luxury homes and neither did the car dealers.

The sale of hand-guns soared and so did the city's murder rate. In 1984 alone there were no less than 17 double murders, five triple slayings and a gruesome quintuple killing – all drug-related.

Image is Everything

But 1984 also brought a positive impact on life in the city and the world's image of it. The weekly television series *Miami Vice*, which starred Don Johnson and Philip Michael Thomas, turned the city's

crime statistics into a pastel-perfect rock video of glamour and intrigue. At first city officials were worried about the damaging public relations effect the show might have. But later, when the glossy images of tropical lushness, beautiful women, fast cars, neon lights, and the downtown skyline were branded into the minds of the TV viewing public across the world, opinions changed; and it was soon realized that *Miami Vice* was in reality giving an essential boost to the flagging local economy.

Miami's crime-ridden reputation was no longer an obstacle to be overcome. It was now considered desirable, enticing and even cool. Tourists from around the world, eager to experience a tame version of the

'Miami Vice', a godsend for the economy

same scenario, came to seek it out, and Miami became one of the hottest, most-talked about cities in America.

Modern Miami

The mid-1980s brought Miami's first Cuban-born mayor, a new, professional basketball team, and a rendezvous for President Ronald Reagan and Pope John Paul II in the gardens of Vizcaya.

The early 1990s brought Hurricane Andrew, which left 150,000 people homeless. Naturally the 2001 terrorist attacks on the US have had a souring effect on American tourism, but it seems Miami will always be a place where people come to play in the Art Deco hotels, dance to sizzling music, and be welcomed by a warm-hearted community.

Historical Highlights

500BC Indians, who likely migrated from the North American northwest, inhabit the verdant areas surrounding present-day Miami.

1513 Juan Ponce de Leon 'discovers' Florida and sails into Biscayne Bay.

1763 The French and Indian War ends, making Florida a British colony after 200 years of Spanish rule.

1784 Britain swaps with Spain, trading Florida for the Bahamas.

1821 The US gains control of Florida and hundreds of runaway slaves settle in the area.

1835 Seminole Indians attack and the bloody 'Dade Massacre' occurs.

1870s Developer William Brickell arrives in Miami and Coconut Grove and establishes the first post office.

1896 Julia Tuttle convinces Henry M Flagler to bring his railroad to Miami. City status conferred on Miami.

1915 Miami Beach becomes a city too, as casinos, cabanas and cafes blossom.

1917 World War I transforms Miami's Dinner Key into a US Naval Air base.

1920s The Roaring Twenties bring a real estate boom, population growth, and modernization.

1926 A brutal hurricane batters Miami, leaving over 100 dead.

1936 Miami hosts the Orange Festival, beginning a tradition of the annual Orange Bowl Parade.

1942 Hotels are transformed into barracks and hospitals during World War II.

1950s The tourism boom brings grand-scale hotels to Miami Beach and the government cracks down on Miami mobsters and illegal gambling halls.

1959 The Cuban Revolution changes the face of Miami when President Fidel Castro declares himself a Communist. Hundreds of thousands of Cuban refugees settle in Miami.

1961 Cuban exiles unite with US agents in the foiled Bay of Pigs invasion of Cuba. Almost 100 people die.

1962 The Cuban Missile Crisis threatens war, and exiles realize that Miami is no longer just a temporary home.

1970s US economic recession affects Miami. President Richard Nixon vacations on Key Biscayne as four Miamians instigate the infamous Watergate political scandal. Thousands of Haitians sail in rickety boats to Miami.

1980 A race riot erupts in Miami over the acquittal of a white police officer accused of murdering a black man. President Castro allows 125,000 Cubans to leave the island and come to Miami, many of them convicted criminals.

1980s The *Miami Vice* TV show premiers. The city elects Xavier Suarez, its first Cuban mayor. President Ronald Reagan meets with Pope Paul II at Vizcaya and the future looks promising.

1992 Hurricane Andrew leaves a trail of destruction.

1997 The Miami-based Florida Marlins baseball team win the World Series, and become the youngest ever champions.

2000 Florida finds itself center-stage as counting and recounting determines the next US president.

2001 The terrorist attacks on the United States take their toll on every state.

The city of Miami sprawls over a large area of land, and since local transportation is less than efficient, the following itineraries have been arranged on the assumption that you have a rental car in the city or some sort of vehicle at your disposal. The only area that is really fit for walking around in is the Art Deco district (Day Two), in which case you may want to start with that tour and rent your car afterwards. Most of the time a sense of direction is easily acquired in Miami if you remember that the ocean is to your east; during the day the location of the sun – which rises in the east and sets in the west – also acts as a guide. Street signs are clearly visible except in the city of Coral Gables where street names are indicated only on tiny, hard-to-read white stones.

All of the best, shouldn't-be-missed parts of Miami have been included in the itineraries which follow, along with some well-kept secret spots which I have selected for you in order to provide a sense of place and make your few days in the city a memorable and worthwhile experience. What is included is an eclectic array of sights and sounds which will, hopefully, make it clear that Miami is much more than just a beach. But of course you must feel free to detour and make your own discoveries.

Downtown Miami and Bayside Marketplace

Morning ride on Metromover. Enjoy the sights of Flagler Street to the Metro-Dade Cultural Plaza. Go past the historical Royal Palm Cottage to the Miami Riverside Walk. Lunch at Bayside Marketplace ($) and explore the shops. Happy hour drinks and snacks at Tobacco Road and the Fishbone Grille.

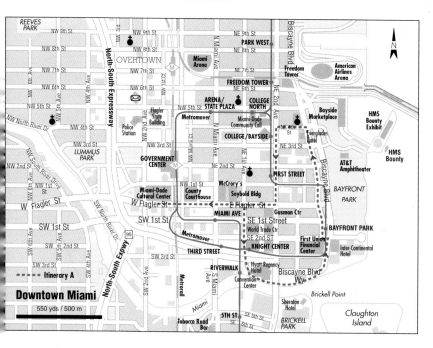

Freedom Tower on Biscayne Boulevard

For our first full-day tour in Miami, put on some sturdy walking shoes and head for the centerpiece of the downtown waterfront – **Bayside Marketplace** (401 Biscayne Boulevard, open daily 9am–midnight, Tel: 577-3344). Public transportation to Bayside is available from most parts of the city, but since today's tour includes stops elsewhere, a car is needed. Bayside can be reached from any of the I-95 downtown exits by driving east to Biscayne Boulevard which runs north and south along the eastern edge of the city. Parking is available in a garage on the northside, and also at meter spots that require coins.

The commercial district of downtown Miami definitely hums with big city intensity. Although less than 100 years old, it has grown to be a bustling metropolis with a dramatic skyline. The afternoon heat can cause the most hearty traveler to wilt, so go walking early and return to Bayside later. After parking the car, walk west (from here it is the only direction possible) on NE 4th Street. To the north stands the **Freedom Tower**, a peach-colored Mediterranean Revival building built in 1925 that once served as a processing center for Cuban immigrants. After walking one block on NE 4th Street you'll come to the **College/Bayside Metromover Station**. Deposit 25 cents in the turnstile and walk up the stairs.

The Metromover offers a terrific over-view tour of downtown. Both the inner and outer loop tracks provide a ten-minute Disney-like ride of dramatic urban views. Stay on the train until it returns

Bayside on Biscayne Bay

Metro Rail over Biscayne

to College/Bayside Station and exit back down the stairs. Continue west on NE 4th Street until you reach NE 2nd Avenue and turn left. In front is the **Wolfson Campus of Miami-Dade Community College**, site of the fall Miami Book Fair. Walk four blocks south until you reach East Flagler Street, the main artery of the downtown commercial district. Turn right and walk four blocks west on Flagler.

The **Walgreen's Pharmacy** on the corner is a classic example of Streamline Moderne architecture. Across the street is the **Gusman Cultural Center**, a glorious Spanish-style theater with a plush and romantic interior. Continuing west on Flagler are dozens of electronic, luggage and jewelry stores. At 169 East Flagler is the **Alfred I duPont Building**, a classic Art Deco office.

At the **Flagler Station mall** at 48 East Flagler Street, stop for an air-conditioned rest. The mall's **Floridita Restaurant**, known in Cuba before its owners moved to Miami, is a good place to stop for a strong cup of Cuban coffee. Heading back onto the street you'll pass the pink and turquoise **Seybold Building**, a mecca for jewelry shoppers. Next door is **McCrory's**, a five & dime store that made history in the 1960s when blacks staged a lunch-time sit-in demanding to be served.

The Courthouse

About one more block and you'll pass the massive, neo-classical **Dade County Courthouse**. Home to the gray suit and briefcase crowd, the courthouse also serves as host to hundreds of turkey buzzards that migrate south each fall and transform the building's angled roof into their winter home. Walking a little further you'll reach the morning destination – the **Metro-Dade Cultural Plaza** at 101 West Flagler. Enter up the ramp alongside the flowing pools of water. The grand, tiled courtyard resembles an Italian *piazza* and is very popular with downtown business people at lunch hour. A small, outdoor refreshment stand sells cold drinks and snacks.

Three beautiful buildings occupy the surrounding grounds: the **Miami-Dade Main Library** (Monday to Saturday 9am–6pm, Sunday 1–5pm) is a good place to browse through a large collection of Florida books; the **Historical Museum of Southern Florida** (Monday to Saturday 10am–5pm, Sunday noon–5pm, reasonable admission charge) maintains a permanent exhibit that explains 10,000

Downtown seen from the mouth of the Miami River

years of South Florida history and includes a simulated ride on a 1920s Miami trolley car, and puts on Florida-related theme exhibits that change every few months; the **Miami Art Museum** (Tuesday to Saturday 10am–5pm, Sunday noon–5pm, reasonable admission charge) is one of South Florida's most respected art museums. Exhibits change regularly and range from American modern to European classics.

After spending some time in the museums and library, continue your walking tour of downtown with your next stop being the Miami River. Due to highway ramps and the curve of the river, the directions here get a little complicated. Go back on Flagler Street and walk east one block to NW 1st Avenue and then turn right. Walk south two blocks to SW 2nd Street and turn left. Walk two blocks again to SE 1st Avenue and turn right. Directly in front is

International Place

the 47-story **International Place**. Designed by the highly acclaimed architect I M Pei, this is a strikingly futuristic chameleon of a building that changes color with the flick of a switch – from pink to blue to green, or whatever suits the occasion.

After walking down SE 1st Avenue for one short block you will notice the **Hyatt Hotel**. The Miami River is behind it so walk toward the rear of the hotel. To the right are eateries situated on the river. You'll also spot a little yellow wooden frame house otherwise known as the **Royal Palm Cottage**. The historic structure built in 1897 once housed the men who worked

22

on the nearby Flagler railroad. Yellow was Henry Flagler's favorite color.

A seawall on the southside of the property runs alongside the **Miami River**. Definitely a working-man's waterway, the river is busy day and night with oil tankers and freighters that connect Florida to the Caribbean and Latin America. Commercial fishing boats also pass in and out and occasionally a sailboat or yacht cruises by. Across the river is the Miami base for the **US Customs Service**. Along its seawall are powerful race boats, once owned by drug smugglers, that have been confiscated and turned into sleek patrol boats.

Stroll under the bridge and down to the end of the **Miami Riverside Walk** and smell the brackish Miami River water get saltier as you get closer to Biscayne Bay. The riverwalk ends at what is now **Biscayne Boulevard** and standing in front is the towering 55-story **Southeast Financial Center**, the tallest building in Florida and one of the tallest in the Southeast. The modern, gray building actually stands atop the site of an ancient Indian burial mound.

Continue walking north along Biscayne Boulevard and follow the signs to Bayside Marketplace. To the right are two more large buildings, the Miami Center and the Hotel Inter-Continental. At 301 Biscayne Boulevard is **Bayfront Park**, a sprawling waterfront park used for outdoor concerts and festivals.

At the southern end of the park is a memorial designed by the late Japanese sculptor Isamu Noguchi and dedicated to the astronauts and crew who lost their lives in the tragic *Challenger* space shuttle explosion. The park also has an amphitheater that puts on night-time laser-light shows throwing beams of bright colors into the Miami sky. Toward the eastern edge of the park stands a statue of Christopher Columbus given to the city of Miami by the Italian government on Columbus Day 1953.

Just north of Bayfront Park are the colorful flags marking the entrance to **Bayside Marketplace**, a festive 16-acre (6.5 hectare) extravaganza of over 140 shops, restaurants and attractions. By now it's time to stop for a late lunch and there are a great many spots to choose from.

At the entrance is **Las Tapas**, a

The Southeast Financial Center

local favorite that offers Spanish dishes and terrific margaritas. Dining is available both inside and at outdoor tables. At the southern end of the first level is **Lombardi's**, an outdoor Italian restaurant featuring live music nightly. At the second-floor **Food Court** you will find dozens of cafeteria-style restaurants with good views of Biscayne Bay and the nearby Port of Miami. Choices are numerous: Greek, Japanese, Italian, Cuban, delicatessen, natural foods, as well as a plentiful selection of sweet treats.

After eating, take some time to wander around Bayside. It usually takes about two hours to explore the entire marketplace. Along the waterfront are docks for commercial and private boats. Live entertainment – music, jugglers, or dancing – goes on day

Sweet treats in the sun

and night by the water's edge. In addition to the larger chain stores dozens of fashion boutiques, jewelry stores and souvenir shops are to be found here. Kiosks, featuring trinkets from around the world, are positioned throughout the lower level. Browse through the Haitian art, Indian fabrics, African wood carvings, and Italian leather goods. One of the more provocative stores (and an enemy of animal rights advocates) is **Art by God**, a shop that sells minerals and gems, bear-skin rugs, stuffed moose-heads, tusks, antlers, and shark jaws.

A few of the more whimsical things to do include posing for a photograph with arms full of live parrots, sitting for a personal caricature drawing, sipping a fresh tropical fruit shake, or indulging in a bouquet of bird of paradise flowers. Alternatively, stop in at the Hard Rock Cafe Miami, part of the international chain, with its emphasis on the city's Latin personality and including memorabilia from local superstars Gloria Estefan and John Secada.

After this Bayside excursion, get back in the car and take in a couple of favorite local bars for happy hour drinks. Once you're out of the parking garage drive south on Biscayne Boulevard, which turns into Brickell Avenue. After crossing the Miami River bridge past the Hyatt Regency Hotel, this stretch of Brickell boasts some of Miami's most colorful and dramatic skyscraper condominiums – one painted a rainbow of colors, another with a huge hole in the center.

Happy hour downtown

At the corner of SE 7th Street turn right and drive one block to Miami Avenue. First stop here is **Tobacco Road** at 626 South Miami Avenue. Free parking is available in the rear of the building; alternatively, meter spots are found in front on the street.

'The Road' as it is called by locals, holds Miami's oldest liquor license and is one of the city's most popular jazz and blues bars. The atmospheric, dark and smoky interior is decorated with old newspaper clippings of articles about the club, and various articles of memorabilia of days gone by.

The late afternoon crowd is usually made up of Brickell Avenue business people stopping for a drink to unwind. Later in the evening (the bar is open until 6am) the place fills up with music lovers and people searching for a cozy and authentic place to hang out. But no matter what time you visit The Road, the atmosphere is always laid-back.

The next stop is the **Fishbone Grille**, located just a few doors away from Tobacco Road at 650 south Miami Avenue. Although this is an authentic, sit-down fish house where the chefs cook with flair in front of the dining patrons, the Fishbone Grille is also a great place to welcome the evening hours by sipping on tall drinks and nibbling on tasty appetizers. Among the favorites here are shrimp-potato fritters, smoked fish mousse, crab cakes, *ceviche*, and *jalapeno* cornbread.

Haitian boats on the Miami River

Miami Beach

Start at MacArthur Causeway. Walk along Ocean Drive with a stop at the Art Deco Welcome Center. Then down Lincoln Road Mall, lunch at the Van Dyke Cafe ($$). Via Washington Avenue to Espanola Way, drinks at The Strand. Dress for the sun, bring some quarters for the parking meter.

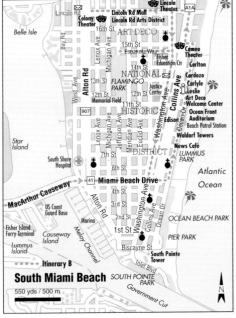

Miami Beach, in the past ten years, has become one of the most colorful neighborhoods in the US. Wandering around its tropical streets, you'll pass some of the most outrageous architecture ever built, along with many eccentric and endearing residents. These days the beach is home to an interesting collection of characters: elderly Jews, young Cubans, New York artists fleeing the cold, fashion models, and some of Miami's trendiest yuppies.

Several causeways link Miami to the barrier island of Miami Beach, but to get to the historic Art Deco district and the fashionable South Beach neighborhood known as SoBe, it's best to take Route 395 east which is accessible from both I-95 and US1. **Watson Island** is on both sides as you drive along the MacArthur Causeway over Biscayne Bay. On the north side of Watson is the **Japanese Garden**, a classic oriental retreat. On the south side is **Chalks International Airline**, the oldest airline in the world. Since the 1930s, Chalks' squat little seaplanes have graced Miami waters with their gooney-bird landings.

Beyond Watson Island to the south is **Dodge Island** and the **Port of Miami**, the world's largest cruise port. During the week there's usually at least one of these floating behemoths in port, but on weekends the line-up of luxury cruise ships – which take over two million passengers a year to the Caribbean – is spectacular. At the

26

Biscayne Bay from MacArthur Causeway

eastern edge of the port is an impressive array of commercial cargo vessels. To the north of Dodge Island are three little gems that serve as posh, private neighborhoods – **Hibiscus**, **Palm** and **Star Islands**. Many of the homes here have yachts moored in front and a few have their own seaplane berths. Palm Island was once the Florida home of the famous American gangster Al Capone.

As the MacArthur Causeway comes to an end, to the right is the **Miami Beach Marina**, a 400-slip basin filled with private sail and powerboats. You are now in Miami Beach. The causeway becomes 5th Street and you'll continue east until you come to **Ocean Drive** and turn left. Driving up Ocean Drive, the wide expanse of white sand and calm blue water – Miami Beach – is on the right. This is the core of the historic **Art Deco district** which technically runs from 6th to 23rd streets along the ocean, and west to Alton Road. The district includes over 500 Art Deco structures.

Drive north on Ocean Drive until you come to 8th Street and begin the task of finding a parking place. The spaces right on Ocean Drive all require quarters for the meters, but there are a few spots on the side streets that are free. Amid the search, you will probably spot a few huge, air-conditioned motor-homes parked in this area catering to the fashion models on photographic shoots.

South Beach

After parking the car, walk along Ocean Drive to take a look at some of the many famous landmarks. At 9th Street is the **Waldorf Towers**, a yellow, purple and white Art Deco hotel with a bright tile veranda. Across the street to the east is **Volley Ball Beach**, where serious and not-so-serious beach lovers like to hang out and play ball. Also on Ocean Drive near 9th at 850 is the **Villa at Cafe Milano**, a charming Italian bistro that is decorated with bold and beautiful artwork. At 10th Street and Ocean Drive is the Edison Hotel, which houses the **Planet Hollywood Ocean Cafe** where hotel guests receive a 15 percent discount on food and soft drinks.

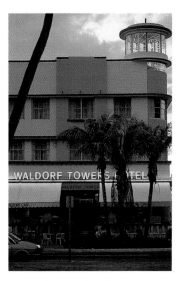

The Art Deco Waldorf Towers Hotel

The cafe includes a bar, restaurant and poolside drinks service where you can sup to your heart's content whilst dipping your toes in the swimming pool. Across Ocean Drive from the Planet Hollywood is the **Miami Beach Ocean Front Auditorium** (Tel: 673-7739). Here, beach residents both young and old gather for music, lectures and lunches.

At 11th Street and Ocean Drive is the **Adrian Hotel**, an Art Deco beauty that caters to a wide range of tourists from across the world. Nearby at 1116 Ocean Drive is **Casa Casuarina**, the magnificent private mansion of the late Italian fashion designer Gianni Versace. It was here, in 1997, that Versace was tragically killed. Formerly a run-down apartment building known as the Amsterdam Palace, the property was bought by Versace in 1992. He had it completely remodeled to its current Mediterranean-style elegance. A sad reminder of an ugly day in Miami Beach history, Casa Casuarina is still owned by the Versace family but its future is uncertain.

The next stop on the route is the **Art Deco Welcome Center** at 1001 Ocean Drive (Monday to Friday 10am–6pm, Saturday 10am–2pm; Tel: 531-3483). Operated by the Miami Design Preservation League, the non-profit preservation group responsible for the movement to preserve the Art Deco properties and listing them on the National Register of Historic Places, the Welcome Center provides a wealth of Art Deco information. It also sells books, souvenirs, postcards, jewelry and Art Deco antiques. On Saturday mornings, walking tours of the district depart from the hotel.

Two of the so-called 'grandes dames' of the Art Deco hotels, are the **Carlyle** and **Cardozo**. Next door, but on Collins Avenue, is the **Cavalier**, considered for years to be one of the most well-managed Deco hotels on the beach. After spending some time at the Welcome Center, continue down Ocean Drive. At the corner of Ocean Drive and 14th Lane is the **Betsy Ross Hotel**, a blue and white colonial structure that looks too Americana and conservative for flamboyant Miami Beach.

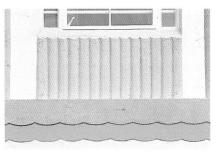

Art Deco detail

One more block will take you to 15th Street where you should turn left and walk one block to **Collins Avenue**. Further north on Collins Avenue is where the grand 1950s Miami Beach hotels such as the **Eden Roc** and **Fontainebleau** are to be found. At Collins Avenue turn right and walk north one more block to Lincoln Road. At the corner of Lincoln Road and Collins Avenue you will see Miami Beach's Art Deco **Burger King**. The historic pink and green structure was transformed into a modern burger joint when the Deco craze swept the SoBe (South Beach) area.

Turn west down **Lincoln Road**, a pedestrian-only thoroughfare. Once thought of as the Fifth Avenue of the South where elegant stores drew shoppers, the **Lincoln Road Mall** has undergone a transition. For years it was neglected and housed only junk jewelry stores and low-grade boutiques. Although many cheap souvenir shops remain, a burst of commercial and artistic energy has revitalized the street, resulting in a number of interesting craft/art shops and nutrition centers. By now, you will probably feel it is time for a snack or lunch break, so before exploring the rest of the

Sunning at the beach

street stop in at the **Van Dyke Cafe**, one of SoBe's popular restaurants, at 1641 Jefferson Avenue (at the corner of Lincoln Road, open daily for breakfast, lunch and dinner). A bustling sidewalk cafe, the Van Dyke offers a variety of omelets, salads, sandwiches, hearty hot dishes and Middle Eastern specialties.

After a little sit-down indulgence, it's back down the street. Lincoln Road is home-base for the **South Florida Art Center**, a collective of almost 100 local artists who share gallery space. Their main office is at 924 Lincoln Road, but there are other galleries in the area exhibiting their work. The New World Symphony, a national training orchestra for young people, perform at 541 Lincoln Road.

Miami City Ballet workout

One of the highlights of the Lincoln Road Mall, which may go unnoticed by the unaware eye, is the headquarters of the **Miami City Ballet** at No 905. Nose prints on the floor-to-ceiling windows suggest that something interesting is going on inside. Here, on almost every weekday, passersby can peer through the windows and see the classical ballet dancers warming up for rehearsals. Under the guidance of director Edward Villella, the ballet company, which was founded in 1986, gained international acclaim amazingly quickly.

After an hour or so exploring the Lincoln Road Mall, head south down the beach. Go back to where you entered Lincoln Road and one block west of Collins Avenue turn right and walk south along **Washington Avenue**. A thriving, commercial street filled with fruit stands, fish markets and tempting bakeries, Wash-

Miami Beach police at work

ington Avenue is where Miami Beach residents go to shop and mingle with their friends.

Walk on down Washington for three blocks until you reach **Espanola Way** where you should turn right. At the corner here stands the Clay Hotel and International Hostel. This striking pink and white Mediterranean-Revival structure is where the Cuban band leader Desi Arnaz made his American debut. The hostel has friendly and helpful staff and is a convivial place for mingling with European travelers.

The rest of Espanola Way is a narrow and beautiful street that looks a lot like a movie set – indeed it featured in many episodes of *Miami Vice*. The pink and white facade with hand-painted tiles runs the length of the street, which is packed with art galleries, boutiques, and vintage clothing shops selling the finest quality goods. After a little shopping on Espanola Way, continue walking south on Washington Avenue. At 11th Street you pass the **Miami Beach Police Station**, an aqua and white streamline structure with a glass brick front.

By now, you are probably in need of a rest, and the last stop on this itinerary is for drinks at **The Strand**, 671 Washington Avenue, about a block away from your car. The Strand is one of the few SoBe restaurant/bars that has survived the fickle Miami bar-going crowd. Its cool and sophisticated decor is unassuming and at first unimpressive. But the mood is relaxing, the drinks are potent, and the hearty American/Continental food is always good.

DAY 3

Coconut Grove

Start with a quick look around Dinner Key Marina, then to Peacock Park. Via Main Highway into the Grove. A tour of the elegant Barnacle house and on to the Bahamian neighborhood. Lunch on Commodore Plaza ($$); Fuller Street for treats and a massage; Coco Walk and Mayfair for boutiques and clubs.

Coconut Grove is an eclectic neighborhood of funky houses, dense natural greenery and a spirited village center that all Miamians love to visit. To get there, drive on Dixie Highway (US1) from either the north or south and turn east at **SW 27th Avenue**. Drive about eight blocks and after crossing South Bayshore Drive enter the **Dinner Key Marina**. Take a loop drive around the marina to get a feel of what live-aboard life in Miami is like. In addition to the many commercial fishing boats that line the entrance to the docks are hundreds of privately owned sailboats and yachts. These moorings are considered prime winter spots for boat travelers and at times there is a waiting list for space.

After cruising through the marina, exit the same way you came in and turn left on South Bayshore Drive. To the left is **Bayside**

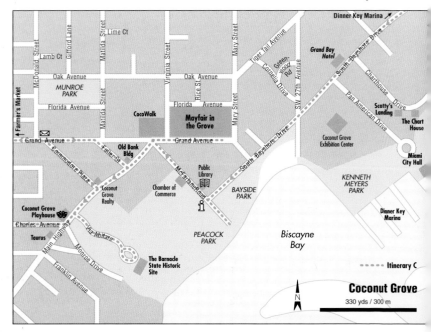

Coconut Grove

330 yds / 300 m

····· Itinerary C

Sleeping after a hard night's fishing

Park, a shady playground dotted with modern sculptures along the perimeter. Park the car where South Bayshore ends and veers to the right to become McFarlane Road. Metered parking places are available at the southern end of McFarlane Road near the water, and also along the street on both sides.

At the southeast end of McFarlane Road is **Peacock Park**, named for the historic Peacock Inn that once stood on this spot. Peacock Park is where families go on weekends to picnic. It also serves as host ground to many Coconut Grove festivals, concerts and food fairs.

Walking up McFarlane (one of the few hills in the city) you'll pass the **Coconut Grove Public Library** at No 2875 (open Monday, Wednesday, Thursday, Saturday 9.30am–6pm; Tuesday 12.30–9pm). Originally opened in 1901, the library has a good collection of books about the area and the tropical, coral rock building is worth a visit. The land was donated to Coconut Grove by Commodore Ralph Munroe, and his wife's grave is in the fenced-in area near the street. Across the street from the library on the left at No 2820 is the **Coconut Grove Chamber of Commerce**.

At the top of McFarlane Road you begin to get into the core area of Coconut Grove. On the right is **Coco View**, a multi-level collection of bars and shops. On the left side are a few interesting finds: the **Catch-A-Wave Surf Shop**, a swimwear and surfboard store. Turning onto Grand Avenue, you'll find two interesting tobacco shops,

Bayside Park

Barnacle State Historic Site

specializing in cigars: **Coco Cigar Shop** and **Yucky's Tobacco and Emporium**.

Turn left where McFarlane Road ends and intersects with **Main Highway**. Down Main Highway you'll pass numerous swimwear shops, yogurt parlors, and outdoor cafes. A few blocks to the south at 3485 Main Highway is the **Barnacle State Historic Site** (Friday to Sunday 9am–4pm, Monday–Thursday tours by reservation Tel: 448-9445). Walk down the deeply wooded entrance road and experience the lush and quiet Coconut Grove of 100 years ago. A nominal entrance fee is required.

The Barnacle was the home of Miami pioneer Commodore Ralph Munroe. Munroe was a naturalist who followed the philosophical path of David Henry Thoreau and the Barnacle shows it. The two-story yellow stucco house constructed in 1891 was built with a natural air-conditioning system of vents and fans. Its wrap-around porch overlooks a broad lawn and catches the breezes off Biscayne Bay. The interior has been kept in its original form, furnished with elegant antiques, lace curtains and oriental rugs.

Goombay Festival

Walk down to the boathouse by the bay and take a look at the *Micco*, a wooden ketch designed and built by Munroe himself. Tours of the house itself are given: call to check the times.

After the tour, leave the Barnacle and continue along the red brick path on Main Highway. One block away cross the street and walk down historic **Charles Avenue**. This is where many of Miami's Bahamian settlers lived while they helped build the old Peacock Inn during the late nineteenth century. The neighborhood remains predominantly Bahamian and not far away is where the annual Miami/Bahamas Goombay Festival is held. At the entrance of Charles Avenue, an historic marker explains the importance of the Bahamian community to the city. Several wooden Bahamian-style cottages of rustic tropical design still line the street.

A one-block walk is all that's needed to get the feel of the neighborhood, after which you head back to Main Highway and walk north. At the corner of Charles and Main is the **Coconut Grove Playhouse** (Tel: 442-4000). Built in 1926, the intimate 1,100-seat theater hosts Broadway plays and serves as a cultural hub for the Grove in winter. Across the street at 3540 Main Highway is **Taurus Chops**. Built in 1922, the building is constructed of Florida cypress and oak beams and has a nautical decor. Formerly a ladies' tea room, the Taurus today is a hit with the Grove's yuppies at happy hour.

Continuing north on Main Highway, our next stop will be **Commodore Plaza**, the Grove's most fashionable street, for lunch. Several outdoor cafes fill up on weekends with people-watchers and posers as college kids cruise with their car stereos blaring. Human-powered rickshaws offer rides. At the corner of Commodore Plaza and Main Highway the **Greenstreet Cafe** and **Mambo's** seafood restaurant compete for the cafe crowds. Next door to the Greenstreet is the **Coconut Grove Flower Shop** that specializes in exotic plants and hand-made wicker baskets.

For lunch, choose between two of the best restaurants on the street. **Anokha ($$)**, at 3195 Commodore Plaza, is a moderately priced family-run Indian restaurant specializing in lamb curry, light snacks and grilled dolphin. Across the street, at 3148 Commodore Plaza, is the **Don Quixote ($$)** restaurant, a Spanish eatery open for lunch and dinner. After a leisurely lunch, continue down Commodore Plaza. On the left side of the street is the **Grove Harbour Courtyard**, a tri-level complex of shops. Also here is the **Sol Gallery**, noted for its collection of fine Haitian art, and **Midori Antiques**, a delightful shop that sells fine Oriental antiques and jewelry.

On the other side of Commodore Plaza are the **Salo Design** shop, a jewelry and art collection from around the world; **This and That Shop**, an authentic thrift shop that has managed to survive the high-rent district of Coconut Grove; and **Trattoria Pam-**

Coconut Grove Farmer's Market

pered Chef, a fine Italian restaurant at No 3145. Commodore Plaza ends at the intersection with **Grand Avenue** and across the street is the **Coconut Grove Post Office**.

If it happens to be the weekend, walk over to the **Coconut Grove Farmer's Market** three blocks west of Commodore Plaza on Margaret Street. This market is a throw-back to the 1960s, complete with organic produce, home-made muffins, natural crafts, music, and a few remaining Grove hippies.

Otherwise, walk north on Grand Avenue and turn right at **Fuller Street**, a one-block-long street dotted with some very off-beat shops. At the intersection of Fuller and Main Highway at No. 3434 is **Joffrey's Coffee Company**, one of the many trendy coffee houses with exotic brews and expensive cookies that have popped up all over the country.

One block south of here, at 3456 Main Highway, you will find the **Christian Science Reading Room** (Tel: 446-2101, Monday to Saturday 10am–4pm). On the street right in front of here is the spot where Coconut Grove's resident minute-massage man sets up shop. The tall, bearded man with the strong fingers is John Balz. His curb-side practice, according to him, can cure all manner of ailments including backaches, headaches, insomnia, and can ap-

A magical one-minute massage on Main Highway

Coco Walk Mall

parently even mend broken hearts.

Walk north on Main Highway to the intersection of McFarlane Road, cross the street and continue on along Main Highway. The multi-level pink and beige complex with the towering palm trees is **Coco Walk** (daily 10am–2am), one of the best hot spots in the Grove. The colorful courtyard often has good live music at night and on weekends.

The shops of Coco Walk offer quality merchandise at reasonable prices. A few large chain stores such as The Gap, Limited Express, and Banana Republic, serve as anchors for the dozens of clever boutiques that occupy the remaining storefronts. Some of the more interesting small stores are the **White House**, a women's clothing store featuring all-white fashions, and **Goodebodies**, an all-natural beauty products shop. At the rear of Cocowalk is an eight-screen movie theater.

The restaurants and bars of Coco Walk are always busy at any time of the day or night. A few of the local favorites are: **Tu Tu Tango**, a French bistro with a vast and inexpensive menu; **Baja Beach Club**, a loud and boisterous club featuring bikini-clad barmaids, and **Hooters**, another let's-get-drunk-and-howl kind of place. And for more intentional late-night laughs, the **Improv Comedy Club** offers local and national stand-up comics.

One block to the north of Coco Walk is another sensational complex of trend-conscious shops, restaurants, and movie theaters – **Mayfair in the Grove**. The centerpiece of Mayfair is **Mayfair House**, a plush 180-room hotel that occupies the top three floors of the complex. On the lower levels are a wide range of upscale boutiques, bookstores and bars including the flashy and loud **Planet Hollywood**, one in the chain of movie memorabilia eateries owned by movie stars Sylvester Stallone, Bruce Willis, Demi Moore and Arnold Schwarzenegger.

Just a few doors away from Planet Hollywood is the staid and serene **Oak Feed Store**, a Coconut Grove hub for natural foods, New Age information and holistic health care. The walkways connecting everything in Mayfair are flamboyant designs of mosaic tiles, copper sculptures and fountains of rushing water.

Dancing at Mayfair House

Morning Itineraries

1. Vizcaya

Vizcaya Museum and Gardens (3251 South Miami Avenue, Tel: 250-9133) in Coconut Grove is a perfect morning excursion.

East facade of Vizcaya villa

South Miami Avenue runs parallel to Brickell Avenue and is less than a mile north of the Rickenbacker Causeway. The entrance to the grounds is clearly marked and free parking is available. Vizcaya (daily 9.30am–5pm), is also accessible by the county's Metrorail and bus systems. Admission fees are inexpensive and well worth the included tour.

Built between 1914 and 1916, Vizcaya was the winter home of American industrialist James Deering. It was the grandest construction project ever attempted in Florida and required over 10,000 laborers – almost 10 per cent of the area's population. The name comes from a Basque word meaning 'elevated place'. Vizcaya was designed to resemble an Italian country villa and appear as if it were 300 years old. Handmade Cuban barrel tiles were imported for the roof; so was European wrought-iron grille work for the gates. Original pilings, dug deep into the ground, saved the structure from collapse during the 1926 hurricane.

During its heyday, Vizcaya occupied 180 acres of land and was a

self-sufficient operation that included stables, a cow barn, poultry house, vegetable garden and pineapple grove. It was staffed with 30 servants. The **70-room palace** sits on the water's edge of Biscayne Bay and is maintained in its original condition complete with millions of dollars' worth of antique European furnishings, art and tapestries. The interior combines Renaissance, Baroque, Rococo and Neo-classical styles. Ground floor rooms are arranged around a central courtyard and include a reception area, banquet hall, tea room, music room, smoking room, and library. Sleeping quarters are on the second floor. The basement, a rarity in Florida, holds the service areas. A well-organized narrated tour available in English, French or Spanish explains all the intricacies of the interior design.

The grounds are dense with manicured **European gardens**, nature trails, and native hammocks that beautifully catch the morning light as it sweeps over the bay. Decorative urns, sculptures and fountains dot the property along with a series of tropically planted

Museum and gardens from the south terrace

islands connected by bridges. A coral rock grotto and swimming pool nestle up to the north side of the palace.

Dade County purchased Vizcaya in 1952, turning it into a museum for the public that now attracts over 250,000 visitors a year. Today it occupies only 10 acres of land, but a pink wall that once surrounded the property still stands along Miami Avenue. A gift shop sells antique jewelry, collectibles and souvenirs. A cafe with indoor and outdoor seating offers a surprisingly good menu of quiche, fresh croissants and robust sandwiches.

Each March, Vizcaya hosts an Italian Renaissance Festival with drama productions, fortune-tellers, court jesters, a life-size chess board that uses people for pieces, and a food buffet that features roast boar and ground 'dragon'.

2. Little Haiti

The neighborhood of Little Haiti is a predominantly black community where many of Miami's Haitian immigrants live. It is surprisingly safe for an inner-city neighborhood, and the area offers an interesting ethnic encounter with a rich and colorful Caribbean culture.

Little Haiti lies within the boundaries of 79th Street to the north, 46th Street to the south, Biscayne Boulevard to the east, and highway I-95 to the west. The best way to get here is to drive along 79th Street coming east from I-95 or west from Biscayne Boulevard. At the intersection of 79th Street and NE 2nd Avenue turn south and hit the heart of Little Haiti's commercial district.

North East 2nd Avenue

First stop is **Les Cousins Book and Record Shop** at 7858 NE 2nd Avenue (daily 10am–6pm, Tel: 754-8452). A large parking lot is available on the south side of the building. Les Cousins is a hub of activity and the best place to find Haitian newspapers and books as well as the largest selections of Caribbean music in Miami; it also has primitive Haitian art and carvings. A lunch counter serves Haitian coffee and sweet treats. Its Haitian owners Viter and Henri Juste are a good source for information on the area.

After Les Cousins, drive south on NE 2nd Avenue until you

40

come to the **Caribbean Marketplace** (Friday and Saturday 10.30am –9.30pm, Tuesday to Thursday and Sunday 10.30am–7pm, Tel: 758-8708) at 5927 NE 2nd Avenue. Its gabled tin roof and bold Caribbean colors of yellow, blue, green and orange are impossible to miss. Parking is available in front. The open-air marketplace was designed to resemble the historic Iron Market in Port-au-Prince, Haiti and was granted the prestigious National Honor Award by the American Institute of Architects in 1991. Intended to be a proud focal point for the neighborhood, it occasionally runs into financial difficulties; as a result, its collection of art galleries, book stores and clothing shops do not always keep reliably regular hours.

If it happens to be Sunday, you should stop in at the **Haitian Catholic Center and Church of Notre Dame D'Haiti** at 110 NE 62nd Street just three blocks away (Tel: 751-6289). The church puts on a beautiful 9am Sunday Mass filled with Haitian music and singing that blends earthy African rhythms with French melodies. Women in colorful silk dresses and men in their finest suits turn out for the spirited weekly celebrations.

Heading south on NE 2nd Avenue again, find a parking spot on NE 54th Street. Most of the small shops in this area are Haitian-owned and cater to a Haitian clientele. There are grocery stores where you'll find Haitian delicacies of dried conch and fresh goat heads along with a wide assortment of sneeze-inducing spices, and Haitian housewives haggling over the price of rice and beans. And more than one *botanica*, phar-

Easter Sunday in Haiti

macies that sell religious paraphernalia and magical herbs for practitioners of the afro-Caribbean religions of *santeria* and voodoo. Although they can be found in most parts of the city, *botanicas* are most common in Little Haiti and Little Havana. Don't be nervous. The atmosphere is a bit unusual but the people are friendly and willing to answer questions. Be open-minded and experiment; stock up on items such as black candles, rosary beads, virility pills, black cat repellent, prosperity spray, serenity salve, bull horns, and rag voodoo dolls.

By now you should be ready for lunch. A few blocks west on what becomes NW 54th Street is one of Little Haiti's most popular restaurants, **Chez Le Bebe** at 114 NE 54th Street, Tel: 751-7368, a comfortable, air-conditioned restaurant serving excellent Haitian food at very reasonable prices. Some of their specialties include *lambi* (stewed conch), *griot* (fried pork), and rum-flavored ox-tail stew, all served with a mixture of rice, beans and fried bananas; a range of beer and wine is also available.

Easter Mass at the Catholic Center

3. The Seaquarium

The Miami Seaquarium (4400 Rickenbacker Causeway, Tel: 361-5705) is a 35-acre bayfront marine park located on the causeway that connects Miami to Key Biscayne. If coming from I-95, take the Key Biscayne exit east a few miles and the park grounds will appear on the right. There's plenty of free parking.

Founded in 1955, the Seaquarium (daily 9.30am–6pm), is one of the world's finest oceanariums dedicated to the research and preservation of sea life. Through the years, it has worked closely with its neighbor the University of Miami's Rosenstiel School of Marine and Atmospheric Sciences. Educational exhibits include marine tanks that house hundreds of species of tropical fish and invertebrates, exotic birds, a rain-forest display, and a stingray pool. A beach wildlife habitat provides a nesting area for a host of native birds, including great blue herons, brown pelicans, cormorants, and flamingos.

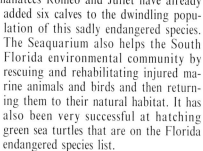

Its manatee (a tropical aquatic mammal) breeding program – the world's first – has produced many manatees conceived and born in captivity. Proud parent manatees Romeo and Juliet have already

added six calves to the dwindling population of this sadly endangered species. The Seaquarium also helps the South Florida environmental community by rescuing and rehabilitating injured marine animals and birds and then returning them to their natural habitat. It has also been very successful at hatching green sea turtles that are on the Florida endangered species list.

Shows that appeal to adults as well as children are offered on a continual basis throughout the day starting at 10am. Entrance fees are moderate with lower rates for children under 12. Early morning hours are usually less crowded than afternoons and, with several things to see, it will likely take between three and four hours to watch the shows and view the exhibits. Lunch and snacks are available and the park's gardens offer many shady spots.

The Seaquarium's main attractions are the shows. The most popular by far is

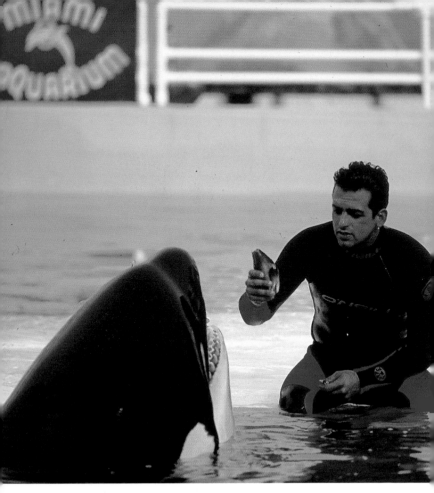

Lolita rewarded for her performance

Lolita the Killer Whale. Weighing in at 8,000lbs, Lolita swims on her back, sprays from her blow hole, waves to the audience with her tail, and shoots out of the water 20ft into the air. Spectators often get drenched by the spray. She also proves to the crowds that killer whales can be affectionate as she kisses her trainers when they feed her tasty fresh fish.

At the **Flipper Lagoon**, the site that once served as the set for two *Flipper* movies and the television series, Flipper – a descendant of the original mammal – and fellow bottle-nose dolphins tail-dance in a choreographed water ballet as their powerful 500lb-bodies sweep back and forth. They also playfully demonstrate their innate sonar skills.

The Seaquarium's glistening Golden Dome serves as the stage for **Salty**, a well-known California sea lion who puts on a flipper-clapping show in which volunteers from the audience take part. Other shows staged regularly include action-packed shark feedings, and underwater fish feedings in an artificial reef tank filled with intrepid scuba divers.

Afternoon Itineraries

4. Key Biscayne

A swim-suit afternoon on Key Biscayne with its Windsurfer Beach, Jet Ski Beach, Hobie Island, and Bill Baggs Cape Florida State Recreation Area; sunset drinks at Sundays on the Bay. Be sure to pack a lunch with drinks, beach towels, dry clothes and plenty of sunblock lotion.

This afternoon is going to be a total play-in-the-water escapade. **Key Biscayne** is a 7-mile-long, 2-mile-wide island paradise just minutes away from downtown Miami. To get there, we'll take the **Rickenbacker Causeway** heading east from either highway I-95 or US1.

Key Biscayne is one of the hundreds of limestone and coral rock barrier islands that lie off the southern end of Florida. Used often by Miami residents who want to get away from the intensity of the city for the day, Key Biscayne is also a residential community that prides itself on its exclusive and expensive waterfront properties. English explorer John Cabot spotted the island way back in 1497 and in 1513 Juan Ponce de Leon claimed the land for Spain. Former US President Richard Nixon called his home on Key Biscayne the 'winter White House'.

After paying the toll to cross over Biscayne Bay, you see the skyline of Miami and the palace of Vizcaya behind you. Coming down from the bridge on the Rickenbacker Causeway, to the left is **Windsurfer Beach**. No signs bear this name, which is actually a local designation, but the rows of pastel-colored sailboards are easily visible by the shore. The calm bay waters and constant east and southeast breezes make this a perfect windsurfing spot. Numerous rental stands offer hourly and half-day rentals with reasonable rates – sophisticated boards for the accomplished and simpler ones for the novice. Most operators will also offer lessons to those who have never tried before.

Jet skiing on Biscayne Bay

Nearby on the north side of the causeway is **Jet Ski Beach**, another no-sign destination. But here also, the line-up of sleek little jet skis will tell you that you have arrived. Jet Ski Beach is one of the few places in the area where motorized skis, banned by local laws in most parts of Miami, are allowed. Rentals

are available by the hour or half-day and rates are reasonable. Life jackets are provided with lessons on how to operate the powerful little machines. Although they're a bit noisy, jet skis are also exhilarating.

A little bit further along the causeway is a popular stretch of beach called **Hobie Island**, which has a thick row of Australian pine trees along the water and several picnic sites to choose from. A row of twin-hulled catamarans (hobie cats) are available for rent and are a good choice for small groups.

If all the action of jet skis, windsurfers and hobie cats is too much, and a deserted beach is more to your liking, continue along the Rickenbacker Causeway past **Virginia Key** and onto the island of Key Biscayne. Once on the key, the causeway becomes Crandon Boulevard. Pass by Crandon Park and head to the very end of the island, past the village area of shops, the Sonesta Beach Resort, and the Key Biscayne Yacht Club for the solitude of **Bill Baggs Cape Florida State Recreation Area**.

The state park was named after newspaper editor Bill Baggs who led a determined crusade to preserve the virgin land. The 400-acre site is considered to have one of the greatest beaches in the eastern US and is the third busiest state park in Florida. The entranceway is a quiet drive past clumps of trees inhabited by rabbits and raccoons. Natural silence is the operative term here and diehard beach-lovers usually fall for it at first sight. Weekends do get a little crowded, but on weekdays it remains a quiet retreat. A small entrance fee for cars is required.

At the farthest end of the park is the red-brick **Cape Florida Lighthouse**, constructed in 1825 to guide sailors. The oldest structure in Miami, the lighthouse has a turbulent past; it was attacked by Seminole Indians in the late 1800s and was later damaged by Confederate sympathizers during the Civil War. Although the interior steps that lead to the top of the tower are closed to visitors, the lighthouse itself is in good shape.

Offshore, the community of stilt houses known as **Stiltsville** can be seen. Unfortu-

The State Park Lighthouse

nately, the offbeat collection of bungalows, standing in the middle of the water, will likely be torn down in the next 10 years because they are considered a nuisance. Also offshore are several man-made reefs that serve as habitats for tropical fish, hard and soft coral, sea anemones, lobsters, crabs, shrimp and sponges. If you packed a snorkel for the trip, now is the time to try it out.

The beach at Cape Florida is glorious – a wide, white swatch of sand with dunes of sea-oats (an endangered plant that must not be picked) and swaying trees in the background. No T-shirt shops or sunglass huts are to be found; it's pure beachfront simplicity. Swimming, sun-bathing and sand-castle building are the main events as pelicans and other water birds float by. Occasionally, stinging jelly fish are hidden in the seaweed, so beware. Restrooms with showers, sinks and water fountains are available free of charge.

After several hours on the beach, put on some dry casual clothes and head off for drinks. Exit the park and drive on Crandon Boulevard until you reach the tranquil restaurant and bar **Sundays on the Bay** (5420 Crandon Boulevard, daily 11.30am–midnight). The nautical feeling of Sundays is always relaxing, and early evening drinks as the sun sets is a great way to end a day.

Rickenbacker Causeway Bridge at dusk

Coral Gables dwelling

5. Coral Gables

Drive along Granada Boulevard to the Biltmore Hotel, then the Venetian Pool down the Miracle Mile for shopping. A drink at Place St Michel and dinner at Norman's restaurant ($$$).

Coral Gables is an enchanting city of Mediterranean-styled architecture, perfectly manicured lawns, and exclusive restaurants and shops. To get there for this afternoon's excursion, drive on US1 and turn west on **Granada Boulevard**, one of the prettiest streets in the city. Although a meticulously managed city, Coral Gables is difficult for the unfamiliar driver to figure out. Its avenues are named after cities in Spain and street signs are small, hard-to-read white corner stones.

Crossing under the Metrorail, the campus of the **University of Miami** will be to your left. The expensive and private university, once mockingly referred to as Suntan-U, has one of the best football teams in the US and a student body of about 14,000. As you drive along Granada, you pass dozens of magnificent Spanish and Italian-styled homes shaded by rows of dense banyan trees.

After driving several blocks and crossing Bird Road, the first stop is the historic Biltmore Hotel. At the intersection of Granada and Anastasia Avenue turn left and drive about two blocks. The 18-story Mediterranean-Revival **Biltmore Hotel** (1200 Anastasia) is on the left and there is free parking available out front. Fashioned after the Giralda Tower in Seville, the Biltmore, built in 1926 and listed on the National Register of Historic Places, was the grand dame of South Florida hotels during the Roaring Twenties. Its swimming pool was the site of the famous Florida water ballets where the rich and beautiful came for fun.

For decades afterwards the Biltmore stood closed and in disrepair. In the 1980s it was restored to its original condition and opened again as a posh hotel in 1987. Since then it's become one of Miami's favorite hideaways for movie stars, fashion models, and politicians and is worth seeking out for a visit. After walking around the hotel grounds, get in the car and drive back onto Anastasia Avenue in the same direction as you originally came. At Granada turn left and drive three blocks until you spot the De Soto Fountain at the center of a circular thoroughfare. De Soto Boulevard is one of the streets that radiate from this circle; turn onto it and drive one block. To your right is the **Venetian Pool** (2701 De Soto Boulevard, hours Monday to Friday 11am–

6.30pm, Saturday and Sunday 10am–4.30pm). Parking is available in front and a modest fee is charged. Handy (and surprisingly, free) maps of Coral Gables with noted historic spots marked on it can be picked up here.

Called the most beautiful swimming hole in the world, the Venetian Pool is a fresh-water coral rock lagoon with caves, waterfalls, and lush landscaping. Its Venetian-styled architecture and soft, sand beach draw hundreds of locals and tourists daily. Since the pool is emptied every single night and refilled early each the morning with fresh artesian well water, a swim here is surprisingly cool.

Once you've experienced the pool, drive on to Coral Way. A few one-way streets make this short drive tricky, so take De Soto Boulevard again about one block and you see Toledo Avenue where you make a left, drive two blocks and cross over Coral Way. In front, at 907 Coral Way is the **Coral Gables House**, locally known as the George Merrick House. This historic beauty with its multi-gabled roof was the home of Coral Gables developer George Merrick. Built in 1899 out of oolite (granular) limestone, the house is now a museum. Although it is only open for tours on Sunday and Wednesday from 1–4pm, visitors can peek in the windows and walk around the grounds any day of the week.

The Biltmore Hotel

Next, drive on Coral Way past many more historic homes until you reach Segovia Street where you should turn right, drive one block to Biltmore Way and turn left. After a few blocks you will come to the intersection of Biltmore Way and LeJeune Road. Here on the left is the semi-circular Spanish Renaissance-style structure that houses the Coral Gables City Hall. Cross over LeJeune Road and here Biltmore Way is transformed into **Miracle Mile**.

The 'mile' as it is called by locals, is a four-block long shopping street of 160 boutiques, art galleries, bookstores, and restaurants. The Gables' most popular shopping district, Miracle Mile is not as glamorous as it likes to think it is, but there are a few fine-quality shops in between rather ordinary stores. Metered parking is available on both sides of the street so find a spot, go for a walk, and explore the neighborhood.

Four blocks north of Miracle Mile is **Place St Michel** at 162 Alcazar Avenue. A 28-room hotel and French restaurant, Place St Michel is one of the finest establishments in the Miami area. Decorated with antiques and bouquets of exotic flowers, its European-style cafe is a lovely place to order a glass of wine and look out the window as the downtown Coral Gables traffic passes by.

After your drink, walk east from the hotel two blocks until you

Miracle Mile City Hall

Mangos

reach Aragon Avenue. Your next stop is **Books and Books** at 296 Aragon (Monday to Saturday 10am–7pm, Sunday noon–5pm). One of the best bookstores in South Florida, this is more than a great place to browse through a fine assortment of tomes. The shop is in a beautiful Mediterranean-styled building with a charming atmosphere, and is where Miami's literary community often congregates for readings and lectures.

Our last stop in Coral Gables is for dinner at **Norman's Restaurant** (Monday to Saturday 6–11pm, $$$) at 21 Almeria Avenue, four blocks south of Aragon. Master chef and cookbook author Norman Van Aken is the main attraction here and his cutting edge eatery is considered one of South Florida's best. Amid a comfortable and subdued atmosphere with an upstairs gallery, patrons come here for the imaginative New World/Caribbean cuisine noted for its unusual, exotic ingredients.

Hotel Place St Michell

6. Little Havana

Lunch at Versailles, then from Woodlawn Park Cemetery to a tropical dream at Kings Cream ice-cream parlor. Visit to Domino Park, the Bay of Pigs Monument and the traditional El Credito Cigar Factory. A peaceful finale at the Miami River Inn and the nearby Jose Marti Park.

Little Havana is the predominantly Cuban neighborhood where English is rarely spoken and the warm Latin culture of the island nation is evident on every corner. The easiest way to get here is to take Flagler Street west from either I-95 or US1. Drive on Flagler until Douglas Road (37th Avenue) where you turn left and travel a few blocks to SW 8th Street, known to Miamians as **Calle Ocho**, where you turn left. Calle Ocho is the main commercial artery of Little Havana, and the site of the outrageous street party called simply 'Calle Ocho'. Held each March, the festival is a 23-block-long salsa-filled bacchanalia of swaying shoulders, grinding hips and supple spines that attracts a million revelers each year and is billed as the largest Latin American festival in the US.

Calle Ocho Festival

Our first stop in Little Havana will be for lunch at **Versailles Restaurant** (3555 SW 8th Street, daily 8am–2am, $). The quintessential Cuban restaurant, Versailles has a wonderfully gaudy atmosphere of crystal chandeliers and wall-to-wall mirrors. Although at lunch time it fills up quickly with local business people, reservations are not required. The food is traditional Cuban home cooking at its best: roast pork, fried plantains, rice and beans, and the restaurant's loud and friendly customers are a good introduction to life in Little Havana. Don't give in to the dessert menu; you must remember to try and save some room for an up-coming ice-cream parlor stop.

Following this rich Cuban meal, return to your car and drive east on 8th Street. A few blocks away, at 3200 SW 8th Street, is the **Woodlawn Park Cemetery**. While some people are uncomfortable about visiting cemeteries, this one offers a lot of insight into the neighborhood of Little Havana. A drive around its scenic and serene grounds shows the impact Cuba's 1959 revolution had on Miami. Buried here in these well-tended graves, in addition to many affluent and important Cuban exiles, are three former presidents of Cuba, as well as Nicaraguan dictator Anastasio Somoza, whose tombstone is marked only with the initials 'AS'. Elderly Cuban women come to the cemetery regularly to place flowers on the graves of their loved ones.

Drive east and pass **Bellas Artes** at 2113 SW 8th Street (Tel: 325-0515). Bellas Artes is a Spanish language theater that caters to

Roadside Cuban sandwiches

Calle Ocho mural

the Cuban community. Its Friday, Saturday and Sunday evening shows are a delight. Productions vary from serious drama to comical farce about the downfall of Fidel Castro. The audience, variously hooting and applauding, is usually as entertaining as the show.

The next stop is **King's Cream** ice-cream parlor at 1831 SW 8th Street (daily 10am–11pm). Free parking is available in front. The assortment of flavors at King's Cream is a tropical dream: guava, mango, coconut, pineapple, papaya – all made from fresh fruit and rich cream.

Leave the car in the vicinity and begin a walking tour. Heading east a few blocks, you pass many shops that once existed in Havana, shops which give a good taste of the Cuban culture. Here are fancy dress stores where mothers shop for their daughters' quince (15th birthday) parties; Cuban coffee stands; bakeries displaying trays of guava-filled pastries; billboards, menus and street signs, all in Spanish; and *gurapo*, which is fresh sugarcane juice sold squeezed to order. In recent years Little Havana has also attracted a good many Nicaraguan immigrants who are claiming their slice of the American pie and their presence in this area is noticable.

Service at the Versailles restaurant

At the corner of 8th Street and 15th Avenue is **Maximo Gomez Park**, better known as **Domino Park**. Here in the fenced-in courtyard, elderly Cuban men gather for a heated game of dominos and talk of the good old days back in Cuba; conversations are usually punctuated with arm-flailing gestures and dramatic outbursts. Park officials enforce a custom that restricts admittance to men over 55, but tourists (including women) are welcome.

On 8th Street near 14th Avenue is a **McDonald's Restaurant**. Now a McDonald's is normally not of interest, but this one sells café Cubano along with *huevo* McMuffins and the entire menu is in Spanish. One more block east on 8th Street near the corner of Cuban Memorial Boulevard (13th Avenue) is the **Bay of Pigs Monument**. The monument, with an ever-burning flame, pays tribute to the men who lost their lives in the foiled invasion of Cuba in 1961. Young Cuban children often come here to place flowers and say a prayer for the homeland they never knew. Just around the corner at

1334 SW 8th Street is **Los Pinarenos**, a Cuban fruit market with the freshest of tropical fruits. Across the street is **Casa de Los Trucos** – House of Tricks. Transplanted from Havana, this neighborhood institution sells costumes, horror masks, magic tricks, and silly toys for grown-ups who like to play.

At the corner of SW 12th Avenue is **La Esquina de Tejas**, the Cuban restaurant that still boasts about the day when President Ronald Reagan stopped in for lunch while on the campaign trail. His photo hangs on the wall. On 8th Street between 12th and 10th Avenues are several *botanicas,* tiny shops that sell religious paraphernalia for both Catholics and those who practice the religion of *santeria,* a form of voodoo. And nearby at 1106 SW 8th Street is **El Credito Cigar Factory** (Monday to Saturday 8am–5pm). El Credito, founded in Cuba in 1907, still has a very old-fashioned philosophy about the art of cigar making. Visitors are welcome to watch as dozens of workers stretch and chop the huge tobacco leaves and then hand-wrap the famous, thick stogies. The atmosphere, complete with antique furniture, is of Havana *circa* 1950. The heady aroma of tobacco hangs in the air. Spanish music plays on the radio as co-workers chatter animatedly together. Boxes of cigars are for sale to take home.

Cigar rolling at El Credito

From here you can either retrace your steps to the car by walking west along 8th Street, or walk one block north to SW 7th Street and take it west instead. SW 7th Street is a mostly residential area and walking along the street you'll pass small apartment buildings and private homes, some with Catholic shrines in the front and live roosters causing a ruckus in the back.

After picking up the car in the parking lot of King's Cream, drive east on 8th Street until you come to 5th Avenue and turn left. Drive about six blocks to SW 2nd Street, turn right and drive one block more. You will

Miami River Inn

now find yourself facing the Miami River – and I suggest that you park the car here on SW South River Drive.

To the left is the **Miami River Inn**, an historic bed and breakfast venue. The newly restored property, listed on the National Register of Historic Places, consists of four wooden buildings built between the years 1906 and 1914. Its 41 rooms are decorated with period antiques, fluffy pastel fabrics and claw-footed enameled bathtubs.

Outside, the grounds surrounding the inn are well worth a look – they offer a surprisingly peaceful and beautiful atmosphere in this otherwise hectic and rather run-down neighborhood.

Across from the inn is **Jose Marti Park**. Named for the revered Cuban writer and patriot, the 10-acre park boasts an Olympic-sized swimming pool, a fountain, a bust of Jose Marti donated by the Cuban government in 1952, and a statue of the late Congressman Claude Pepper. A maze of red-brick walkways leads down to the river's edge, where rusty old freighters piled high with stolen bicycles await their journey to the Caribbean. A dramatic view of the Miami skyline serves as a backdrop. The park is normally filled with children playing and mothers pushing baby carriages during the day, but it can take on a slightly menacing character after nightfall.

Jose Marti Park

Cauley Square

7. Southern Attractions

South Dade County was ravaged by Hurricane Andrew in 1992, but over the years has come back to life. Tour an area of exotic plants and wild animals, and visit Miami Metrozoo.

The southern end of Dade County bore the brunt of Hurricane Andrew as it ripped through South Florida in August, 1992. At the time the worst natural disaster in American history, the 160-mph winds which left the city of Miami miraculously intact slammed through this region with devastating power, flattening wooden buildings, uprooting trees, destroying homes and attractions, and causing serious damage to the agricultural fields that had for decades previously put Dade County among the top 100 fruit-and-vegetable producing counties in the United States. In the aftermath of the hurricane, however, South Floridans were determined to rebuild. With the help of the Red Cross, over 7,000 military troops, and monies received from all over the world, South Dade County was and still is undergoing massive restoration. The state and US governments were determined to get the "Sunshine State" back on its feet immediately, and for the most part they have succeeded. Despite the scars that can still be seen – usually away from the main roads – the area has several family-oriented attractions that make for a pleasant day out.

Orchids are not uncommon here

56

To get to this region, drive south on US1, which is locally called South Dixie Highway, to SW 224th Street. From downtown Miami it will be about a 40-minute drive. The first stop is **Cauley Square**. A former railroad town, Cauley Square is a romantic little enclave reminiscent of pre-World War II Florida. The cluster of houses were built by Miami pioneers who worked with Henry Flagler when he built the original highway that links Miami to Key West. Intense efforts directly after the hurricane ensured that everything was reconstructed with authenticity, and it was only a matter of time before the **Tea Room at Cauley Square** was again the perfect place to stop for lunch.

The Tea Room is like a visit to grandmother's house. A cozy dining area with several rooms, it is graciously decorated with lace table cloths, crystal glassware and antiques scattered everywhere. The surrounding ten acres of Cauley Square house over two dozen specialty shops that include antiques and books, vintage clothing, Florida art, pottery, flowers, gems and crystals, a perfumery, toy store, bakery and aviary.

The countryside in this part of Florida is where blue jeans, straw hats and pick-up trucks are more in vogue than the designer clothes, pink cocktails and fancy white convertibles found in Miami Beach. Recreational vehicles and trailer parks are also a common feature on the landscape. The land all around Cauley Square is a fertile agricultural belt that represents a $200-million-yearly industry for Dade County and supplies vegetables in winter for much of the United States. There are also lots of pick-your-own fruit fields scattered around, should you and/or the kids want to stretch your legs and fill your stomachs at the same time.

Along with tomatoes, peppers, cucumbers and squash, there are several exotic fruit and spice farms that produce such specialties as ginger, coriander, papaya and mangos. One particularly exotic farm

Rural dwelling now destroyed

was the Orchid Jungle, a plant lover's paradise where blossoms from every part of the world were raised and sold. Alas, the evil force of Hurricane Andrew combined with the good fortune of the owner (who won the lottery), and Orchid Jungle closed down for good. Hopefully, the beautiful grounds will be made into a public park.

There is another kind of jungle nearby, however. Once you get to SW 216th Street, turn right. After a few blocks you should begin to see the signs for **Monkey Jungle** (tel: 235-1611, moderate entrance fee). One of Miami's oldest animal attractions, its unique selling point is that humans are in cages while the monkeys run freely. At 30-minute intervals there are also various animal shows.

North of Monkey Jungle is the **Miami Metrozoo** (12400 SW 152nd Street, daily 9.30am–5.30 pm, Tel: 251-0400, moderate entrance fee; last ticket sold at 4pm.). To get there, drive east on SW 216th Street until you come to SW 147th Avenue, turn left and drive north to SW 152nd Street, turn right and drive until you see the entrance to the zoo.

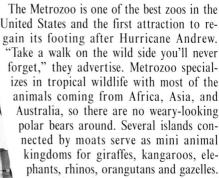

Metrozoo

The Metrozoo is one of the best zoos in the United States and the first attraction to regain its footing after Hurricane Andrew. "Take a walk on the wild side you'll never forget," they advertise. Metrozoo specializes in tropical wildlife with most of the animals coming from Africa, Asia, and Australia, so there are no weary-looking polar bears around. Several islands connected by moats serve as mini animal kingdoms for giraffes, kangaroos, elephants, rhinos, orangutans and gazelles.

An elevated monorail and a narrated tram tour offer an overview of the zoo's vast grounds, while **Paws**, a petting zoo for children, allows youngsters to touch and learn about all the animals. Kids also make a bee-line for the state-of-the-art playground.

A tropical rainforest environment has at one time or another been the home to over 300 rare and exotic birds. But birds are only part of the attraction at Metrozoo: other popular characters include a family of rare white bengal tigers, and three Australian koala bears named Muesli, Sydney and Koobear – Miami's favorite marsupials who even had (pre-hurricane) their own grove of eucalyptus trees to munch on. The koalas adapted so well to Metrozoo that in 1989 they produced a cub, the first koala birth in the United States outside of California.

1. The Everglades

Down the Tamiami Trail to Coopertown's for an airboat ride. To Everglades Safari Park for man-created attractions. Miccosukee Restaurant for a native American Indian lunch ($) followed by a tour of Miccosukee Village. Finally to Shark Valley, for a glimpse of the wild.

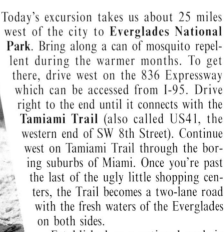

Today's excursion takes us about 25 miles west of the city to **Everglades National Park**. Bring along a can of mosquito repellent during the warmer months. To get there, drive west on the 836 Expressway which can be accessed from I-95. Drive right to the end until it connects with the **Tamiami Trail** (also called US41, the western end of SW 8th Street). Continue west on Tamiami Trail through the boring suburbs of Miami. Once you're past the last of the ugly little shopping centers, the Trail becomes a two-lane road with the fresh waters of the Everglades on both sides.

Established as a national park in 1947, the Everglades is actually a shallow, slow-moving river that looks like a wet carpet of grass. Its charms are subtle and first-time visitors are often disappointed by the lack of drama in the landscapes. About 100 miles long and 50 miles wide, the Everglades represents an ecosystem that supports hundreds of species of animals including alligators, crocodiles, manatees, deer, otters, storks, turtles, and bald eagles. Within it are copses of hardwood trees, dense pine forests and thick mangrove swamps, and it provides a glimpse of the earth's prehistoric past. The Everglades is also essential to life in South Florida

because it provides the bulk of the area's water supply. But sadly it is going through hard times these days; pollution from farm chemicals has seeped into the water, and urban developments continue to nibble away at its borders.

Our first stop on Tamiami Trail will be for a morning airboat ride at **Coopertown's** (daily 8am–7pm, Tel: 226-6048). Although there are several operators who offer airboat rides, Coopertown's is one of the best. The powerful flat-bottom boats glide across the Glades and into the dense swamp for an exhilarating 30-minute ride. The guides provide background information about the Glades and usually stop to feed marshmallows to their favorite alligators. Fees are very reasonable and ear-plugs to exclude the motor noise are provided.

After this journey through the wetlands, continue along the Trail and on to **Everglades Safari Park** (daily 8.30am–5pm), a major tourist attraction that hints of Disney-like commercialism. Diversions here include a wildlife museum, alligator wrestling, boat rides, and nature trails. Admission fees are moderate.

An inhabitant of the Everglades National Park

Traditional Miccosukee fabrics

The next stop on the Trail is the **Miccosukee Restaurant** (open daily) for lunch. Situated on the banks of the water, the large wooden structure also houses an Indian information center. The food on offer is native American Indian style: frogs' legs, catfish, pumpkin and Indian fry bread. After lunch drive about a mile further and stop at the **Miccosukee Indian Village** (daily 9am–5pm). Here, the Florida tribe puts on an informational display along with the requisite alligator wrestling shows.

The Miccosukees branched off from the Florida Seminole Indians many years ago and were recognized by the US government in 1962 as an official native American tribe. Like most others, they are trying to maintain as much of their heritage as possible. Tours of the grounds highlight the native Indian lifestyle and language. A gift shop sells crafts: pottery, moccasins, beaded jewelry, and traditional Miccosukee brightly colored patchwork fabrics. Admission fees are moderate.

For the last stop, go back on the Trail but this time head east for a late afternoon visit to **Shark Valley** (daily 8.30am–6pm, moderate entrance fee, Tel: 221-8455). Part of Everglades National Park and located on the headwaters of the Shark River, Shark Valley is a recreation area with a helpful Everglades information center. The secluded and protected land is a good place to spot alligators, snakes, turtles, and rare birds. A 15-mile loop road can be explored by taking one of the ranger-narrated tram tours, renting bicycles, or on foot. A wooden observation tower offers an excellent bird's-eye-view of the groups of hardwood trees and surrounding islands.

2. Key Largo

Overseas Highway to Key Largo. Visit the Caribbean Club and 'African Queen', both made famous by the movie industry. After lunch visit the first underwater state park in the US, John Pennekamp. Dinner at Crack'd Conch ($). Be sure to pack a swimsuit, towels, and sun-block lotion before setting out.

The Florida Keys are a string of sultry islands surrounded by some of the clearest waters in the northern hemisphere. The upper Keys are about a 1½-hour drive from Miami and make a relaxing day trip. To get there, take the Florida Turnpike which lies west of the city and drive south until it ends and becomes US1, known in the Keys as Overseas Highway.

Driving south, to the left of the highway is the Atlantic Ocean, to the right the Gulf of Mexico. Little green mile markers are posted throughout the highway with MM 0 being Key West, the southernmost island. The drive takes you past dozens of small motels, marinas, shell shops, seafood restaurants and tranquil views of the waters.

As you cross the Jewfish Creek bridge, you officially enter the Keys and the northern end of Key Largo. Originally called Rock Harbor, the island decided to capitalize on the success of the romantic Humphrey Bogart and Lauren Bacall movie *Key Largo* which was filmed here (and on a stage in Hollywood). It changed its name in 1948.

Our first stop on US1 is the **Carib-**

The Caribbean Club

bean Club at MM 104. The club was used for the interior scenes of *Key Largo*, and today is a good-old-boy neighborhood bar. Posters and photographs from the movie hang on the otherwise ordinary walls. Out back is a group of picnic tables with a salty-smelling vista of the Gulf. Although the sign out front says open 24 hours, locals know that operating hours are more likely 7am–4am.

After checking out this famous, but somewhat run-down spot, continue driving south on the highway until you come to the **Holiday Inn Key Largo Resort** at MM 100. Here, in the hotel's Harbor Marina, is a little more movie memorabilia – the original 30-foot boat *African Queen* used by Katherine Hepburn and Humphrey Bogart in the John Huston film of the same name. The steam-powered wooden craft is actually used to take tourists on 30-minute cruises down a canal and out to the ocean; the expensive fare doesn't stop classic film buffs who can't resist the opportunity. After ogling the venerable old 'Queen,' stop in at the Holiday Inn restaurant for an early lunch.

Following lunch, drive back north on US1 to MM 102 and this afternoon's destination, **John Pennecamp Coral Reef State Park** (daily 8am–sunset, Tel: 451-6322, an entrance fee of a few dollars is required at the gates). The first underwater state park in the US, Pennecamp is a 178-square-mile ocean refuge of mangrove swamps, coral reefs and vast seagrass beds. The grounds of the park proper include mangrove walkways, a snack and gift shop, a canoe beach, and an air-conditioned visitor center with educational marine exhibits.

The highlight of the park, however, is the reef that lies about five miles offshore. Inhabited by a vast eco-system of seafans, shrimp, moray eels, sponges, coral, and over 650 species of tropical fish, the reef attracts both experienced and novice divers. Man has added to its intrinsic natural beauty with an eery, 9-ft-high bronze statue called *Christ of the Deep* which can be seen 20 feet below the surface.

Glass-bottom boat tours leave from the park's grounds throughout the day, as do snorkeling and scuba diving trips out to the reef. Equipment hire on the spot ranges in price from $10 to $100, depending on the sophistication of the items used.

Following an afternoon out on the reef, and changing into some dry clothes, begin your drive back to Miami, but first take the opportunity to stop at a favorite local restaurant for a seafood dinner.

Exiting Pennecamp, turn right and drive north to MM 105 for the pleasures of the well-known **Crack'd Conch** restaurant (closed Wednesday, Tel: 451-0732).

Conch (here pronounced 'conk') is not only an edible mussel found in the Florida Keys, it's also the name used for locals who were born in the Keys, many with ancestral ties to the nearby Bahama Islands. The Crack'd Conch, housed in a gingerbread-like cottage with a bamboo interior, serves area specialties like conch fritters, conch chowder and fried fish, along with over 80 types of cold beer. A meal here makes a perfect end to a Key Largo excursion.

Secrets beneath the surface

'What is the best thing to buy and bring home from a trip?' is the classic question asked by many travelers. In Miami, shopping usually means designer clothes and electronic gadgets. Or even rubber alligators or cans of sunshine. But there are a few exceptions.

The Miccosukee Indian Village west of the city on the Tamiami Trail sells the most 'native' souvenirs you'll find – hand-sewn clothing made of fabric that is woven together from bits of colorful cloth. The patchwork jackets, dresses, skirts and shirts can be beautiful.

Then there are the hand-rolled cigars of Little Havana. Transplanted to Miami with the first wave of Cuban refugees who settled in the city, Cuban cigars are potent and intoxicating and not to be taken lightly. They are produced at El Credito in a small storefront on SW 8th Street and – with some evening cognac – serve as a sweet reminder of your visit.

The traditional shopping malls and arcades of Miami are not only full of locals buying so-called necessities, but are also busy with shoppers from the Caribbean and Latin American countries who travel to the city with empty suitcases searching for bargains and things they can't obtain at home. Swimwear and beach clothes are good value for any visitors.

Following are a few popular places for all sorts of shopping, most of which are open seven days a week.

Bayside Marketplace

On the waterfront downtown, Bayside is a flashy outdoor arcade full of neon signs and impulse items. There are over 100 shops,

Santeria symbol, Little Havana

kiosks, and dozens of restaurants. A good place for clever little knick-knacks to take home to friends.

Bal Harbour Shops

North of Miami Beach in the exclusive city of Bal Harbour, this indoor mall specializes in small designer shops like Gucci, Cartier, FAO Schwarz and Fendi along with the larger chains of stores like Neiman Marcus and Saks Fifth Avenue. It's also a good place for beauty products and facials. (Parking fee.)

Cauley Square

South of Miami on US1, Cauley Square (see *Pick & Mix* 7, page 57) is an eclectic collection of Florida antique and craft shops, art galleries, an exotic bird aviary, bakery and cozy little tea room. (Closed Sunday.)

Dadeland Mall

A mall of major magnitude, Dadeland has five anchor stores and over 170 specialty shops for shoes, accessories and jewelry, along with a bazaar of international foods. A practical place to find quality clothing at easily affordable prices.

Downtown Miami

In the area of Flagler Street and South Miami Avenue are literally dozens of small electronic and jewelry stores that draw hundreds of South American and other shoppers every day. The best buys are in radios, stereos, video cassette recorders, computers, television sets, gold chains and designer sunglasses. All the stores are closed on Sunday.

Espanola Way

In South Miami Beach, Espanola Way features a group of art and antique galleries and a few vintage clothing shops that make funky dressers swoon. Nearby are lots of cafes and inexpensive Cuban restaurants. (Closed Sunday.)

The Falls

In southern Dade County, the Falls is an up-scale shopping center with waterfalls cascading

Flower vendor in Coconut Grove

over a fresh-water pond. It houses Bloomingdale's, a good sporting goods store, and trendy boutiques like Banana Republic and Victoria's Secret.

Mayfair/CocoWalk

Side-by-side, these two shopping centers draw thousands daily into the heart of Coconut Grove. Mayfair offers expensive specialty European boutiques, CocoWalk has more affordable but just as desirable goodies.

Miami Design District

A collection of show rooms that feature interior decorations ranging from Art Deco furniture to tropical fabrics. Located from NW 36th to 41st streets between NE 2nd Avenue and North Miami Avenue (closed Sunday).

Miracle Center

In Coral Gables on Coral Way, this big, ugly modern building houses several levels of specialty shops and movie theaters with a good selection of blue jeans, sunglasses, and casual clothes. (Parking fee.)

Cuban market in Little Havana

Omni International Mall

Housed inside downtown's Omni International Hotel, this mall has two levels of major department stores, dozens of boutiques, several restaurants, and a carousel and entertainment center for children. (Parking fee.)

Eating

Miami's dining choices are a unique melange of flavors that include Caribbean and Latin American ethnic, Southern-style home cooking, and a touch of kosher tradition. Tropical ingredients, plucked fresh from the area, are at the heart of most menus. Seafoods – especially grouper, snapper, stone crabs and shrimp – are a good choice. Exotic fruits – papaya, guava, coconuts, mangoes – make their way into everything from desserts to drinks.

Cuban food, often written in Spanish on menus, has become a Miami staple. A few of the common dishes are: *morros y cristianos* – black beans and rice, *calabaza* – sweet squash, *plantanos* – fried bananas, *picadillo* – ground beef with olives served over rice, *flan* – a sweet, rich custard. Cuban coffee is served strong and sweet in tiny cups and can be found almost everywhere.

From Jamaica are specialties like curried goat and spicy meat patties. From the Bahamas come conch fritters and conch salad. With Miami's large Jewish population, it is hardly surprising that area's delicatessens serve the best chopped liver, *matzoh* ball soup, and hot pastrami on rye south of New York City. And then there are the indigenous specialties of fried alligator and Key lime pie, a light, fluffy dessert pie made with local limes.

The listing on the following pages is a selection of the city's best restaurants and cafes. The price range is rated accordingly: $ – less than $20, $$ – $20–30, $$$ – over $30 for an average meal for one, excluding drinks or wine.

Breakfast

GREENSTREET CAFE ($)
3468 Main Highway, Coconut Grove
Tel: 444-0244
A lively outdoor cafe in the Coconut Grove area. Pets and well-behaved children are welcome, and the menu features fresh fruit salads, omelets, granola, bagels and muffins.

JJ'S AMERICAN DINER ($)
101 Aragon Avenue
Coral Gables
Tel: 448-6886
Thick French toast, yummy pancakes, crispy bacon. Recommended for an authentic, traditional all-American breakfast experience.

News Cafe ($)
2901 Florida Avenue
Tel: 774-6347
This 24-hour cafe bustles with trade and its menu stands the pace. Home-style breads and muffins, bowls of granola, sizzling omelets.

Wolfies ($)
19501 Biscayne Boulevard
Tel: 682-9653
Endless coffee, baskets of bagels, and perfectly prepared eggs. A local Jewish deli tradition.

Lunch

Big Fish 2000 ($)
55 SW Miami Avenue
Downtown Miami
Tel: 373-1770
Smack on the Miami River, Big Fish 2000 is about as local as you can get. Fish sandwiches, chowders and cold beer.

Brickell Emporium ($)
1100 Brickell Plaza
Downtown Miami
Tel: 377-3354
A popular lunch hang-out with the downtown business crowd. Quick service and hearty food.

Chez Le Bebe ($)
114 NE 64th Street
Tel: 751-7369
Excellent Haitian food at reasonable prices.

Fuddruckers ($)
3444 Main Highway
Coconut Grove
Tel: 442-8164
Burgers, thick sandwiches, and heaping French fries with a second-floor view of all the Grove action. Also at 7800 SW 104th Street, Tel: 274-1228.

Johnny Rockets ($$)
3036 Grand Avenue
Coconut Grove
Tel: 444-1000
A 1950s style diner complete with jukebox music, serving juicy hamburgers, sandwiches and thick milkshakes. Also at 8888 SW 136th Street, Tel: 252-8181.

Larios on the Beach ($$)
820 Ocean Drive
Miami Beach
Tel: 532-9577
Owned by local singer Gloria Estefan, Larios is a classic sidewalk oceanfront cafe with satisfying Cuban cooking and great-people watching. Becomes a salsa club after dark.

Norma's on the Beach ($$$)
646 Lincoln Road
Miami Beach
Tel: 532-2809
An offshoot of a well-known restaurant in Jamaica, Norma's offers elegant Caribbean fare such as pumpkin soup, snapper in lime sauce, rum cake and, of course, the famous Blue Mountain coffee.

Versailles ($)
3555 SW 8th Street
Little Havana
Tel: 444-0240
The quintessential Cuban restaurant – gaudy decor, lots of noise and delicious food. Pitchers of sangria and hearty white bean soup.

Dinner

Akash of India ($)
173 Sunny Isles Boulevard
North Miami
Tel: 947-8672
Indian curries, vegetarian cuisine and delicious hot breads from a tandoori oven.

Caffe Bolla ($-$$)
1717 N. Bayshore Boulevard
Tel: 371-9055
This small, 40-seat restaurant serves first-rate home-made Italian food.

Capitol Grille ($)
444 Brickell Avenue
Tel: 374-4500
A masculine environment with dark-wood paneling and stuffed animals on the walls. Portions are suitably hearty.

China Grill ($$$)
404 Washington Avenue
Tel: 534-2211
Pan-Asian innovative cuisine served in glitterati environment.

Joe's Seafood ($)
400 NW N River Drive
Miami.
Tel: 374-5637
A rustic Miami River fish-house with a Cuban flavor. Gourmet chefs prepare a range of seafood delights to suit all tastes.

John Martin's ($$)
253 Miracle Mile
Coral Gables
Tel: 445-3777
An elegant Irish pub that specializes in steak-and-kidney pie, grilled lamb, corned beef and cabbage and York-shire pudding. Has an assortment of Irish whiskies.

Original Caribbean Kitchen ($)
16894 S. Dixie Highway
Tel: 252-1229
True to its name, this small restaurant offers traditional rice and pork dishes plus fried plantain and beans.

Le Provencal ($$)
382 Miracle Mile
Coral Gables
Tel: 448-8984
Delicious French and Mediterranean cuisine is served by attentive and knowledgable staff.

The Place For Steak ($$)
1335 79 Street
North Bay Village
Tel: 758-5581
A New York steak-lovers' delight. Numerous fresh cuts of prime beef to choose from.

Puerto Sagua ($)
700 Collins Avenue
Miami Beach
Tel: 673-1115
A down-home and very local eatery with heaping portions of delicious Cuban cookery.

A warm Miami welcome

Sakura Gables($)
440 S. Dixie Highway, Coral Gables
Tel: 665-7020
A friendly *sushi* bar with good *miso* soup, *tempura* and *teriyaki*.

Señor Frogs ($)
3480 Main Highway, Coconut Grove
Tel: 448-0999
A funky indoor/outdoor place with good Mexican food and delicious, icy margaritas.

Sport Cafe ($$)
560 Washington Avenue, Miami Beach
Tel: 674-9700
Real Italian food served in a relaxed and cozy atmosphere.

Tani Thai ($$)
12269 S. Dixie Highway
Tel: 253-3583.
An extravagant dining experience offering the finest selection of Thai specialities. The decor is elegant.

Thai Orchid ($$)
317 Miracle Mile, Coral Gables
Tel: 443-6364
Perfectly seasoned Thai food in a calm setting of orchid plants and soothing music. Reservations are necessary.

Victor's Cafe ($$)
2340 SW 8th Street
Tel: 541-5416
One of Miami's Cuban restaurants that takes traditional cooking one step further.

Miami has come a very long way from the years when the only nightlife consisted of a low-grade comedy act at some big, beach-front hotel.

The Arts

The classical music season in Miami runs from October to May. The area's finest is the **Florida Philharmonic Orchestra**. Their repertoire ranges from classical symphonies to outdoor popular concerts under the stars, 243 University Drive, Coral Gables, Tel: 476-1234. The **New World Symphony** is an advanced training orchestra for gifted young people, 541 Lincoln Road, Tel: 673-3330. The **Florida Grand Opera** features artists from around the world, Tel: 250-5277, and the **Miami Chamber Symphony** offers classical concerts usually held on the University of Miami campus, Tel: 858-3500.

Thanks to the artistic direction of Edward Villella, the finest American-born ballet dancer in the country, the **Miami City Ballet** adds exuberance to the city's cultural scene.

Downtown after dark

The Latin-flavored company combines classical ballet with bits of tango and jazz and is sure to provide an evening of fine entertainment. They're in Miami October to May, 905 Lincoln Road, Miami Beach, Tel: 532-4880.

Theater

There are several theaters scattered throughout the Miami area and performances are listed in local newspapers. **The Coconut Grove Playhouse** (3500 Main Highway, Tel: 442-4000) offers intimate

Miami City Ballet

theater from October to June in an historic 1920s Spanish Rococo building. The **Florida Shakespeare Theater** (1200 Anastasia Avenue, Coral Gables, Tel: 445-1119) is home to several theater companies and hosts the annual Florida Shakespeare Festival and the Hispanic Theater Festival. It is open from September to June.

The **Jackie Gleason Theater of the Performing Arts** (1700 Washington Avenue, Miami Beach, Tel: 673-7300) is a modern, 1800-seat theater locally known as TOPA that features major Broadway productions September to May. The **Colony Theater** (1040 Lincoln Rd, Miami Beach, Tel: 674-1026) is a much cozier theater in the Art Deco District that specializes in offbeat drama, dance and musical productions.

Evening Cruises

Miami offers a wide variety of night-time nautical excursions, from romantic dinner cruises with candles and wine, to deep-sea fishing charters that troll for big game shark. Prices range from a $10 per person sailing cruise to around $500 per night for a private fishing charter. Following are a few of the finest:

Dinner Cruises

CELEBRATION–FLORIBBEAN
HOSPITALITY CRUISES
*3239 W. Trade Avenue, Suite 9,
Coconut Grove.
Tel: 445-8456.*
The *Celebration* and the *Floribbean*

are 150-passenger party yachts that offer evening trips. Three decks high and 92-ft long, the *Celebration* has an air-conditioned lower deck with large windows, a full liquor bar and a canopy-covered outdoor dance floor. Sit-down dinner cruises are available that usually depart from Bayside Marketplace at 5pm and return at 7pm. The boat also offers a narrated 1½ hour cocktail sightseeing cruise Tuesday to Sunday through what Miami calls its millionaire's row of waterfront homes.

CARNIVAL CRUISES
*3655 NW 87th Avenue
Tel: 577-8200.*
Carnival offers exciting cruises to the Bahamas and Caribbean. Call for more information about short tours and trips that may require only a day or two on the ship.

Evening on the 'Tropicana'

ISLAND QUEEN
401 Biscayne Boulevard
Bayside Marketplace
An area institution, the *Island Queen* has been specializing in waterway tours of Miami for over 40 years. The double-decker, 75-ft passenger ships offer Friday to Saturday night tours of the city's skyline and millionaire's row. Tours are narrated in English and Spanish and depart at 7.30 and 9.30pm. They also have Friday to Saturday disco music trips that depart at 9.30 and 11.30pm.

STAR CLIPPERS INC.
4101 Salzedo Avenue
Tel: 442-0550
www.starclippers.com
For those who have never been on a real cruise, Star Clippers offers a taste of the ocean liner experience in their popular short cruises. Sailing

out of Miami Beach, the boats are like a Noah's Ark in their varied cast of characters. Grandmothers, gamblers, teenagers, families, tourists and lovers all take part.

Bars/Clubs
The legal drinking age in Florida is 21, and some form of identification is often required for entrance. Closing times for bars range from midnight through to 6am. Unless you are visiting one of the more sophisticated establishments, dress is usually fairly casual.

THE ABBEY BREWING COMPANY
1115 16th Street
Miami Beach
Tel: 538-8110
You won't find any fashion models or trend-setters swanning around the Abbey Brewing Company, just lots of discerning locals who come regularly to sample the best home-brewed beers in the area.

CAFE NOSTALGIA
432 NW 41st Street
Miami Beach
Tel: 695-8555
This small, smoky saloon dedicated to old-time Cuban singing stars, features some of the finest live Cuban acts in town. The continuously-shown archive movie clips of Havana add to the venue's interesting and evocative atmosphere.

CLUB DEUCE BAR & GRILL
222 14th Street
Miami Beach
Tel: 531-6200
A colorful neighborhood liquor bar full of bizarre characters. Serious drinkers usually feel at home; unadventurous types, however, might feel intimidated.

Doc Dammers Saloon
180 Aragon Avenue
(Colonnade Hotel)
Coral Gables
Tel: 441-2600
An elegant and sophisticated hotel speakeasy for grown-ups.

The 1800 Club
1800 N Bayshore Drive
Miami
Tel: 373-1093
A smoky neighborhood bar that time forgot, the 1800 club is where local journalists, lawyers, cops and politicians come to unwind.

Martini Bar
3390 Mary Street
Tel: 444-5911
As the name suggests, this location lends itself to long spirit-supping and sheer pleasure. A number of other venues in the same building make this a good place to start an evening out.

Murphy's Law Irish Pub
2977 McFarland Road
Coconut Grove
Tel: 446-9956
Murphy's Law offers a real taste of Ireland in the heart of Coconut Grove,

Dancing in Coconut Grove

with imported beers and a traditional Irish menu.

Power Studios
3701 NE 2nd Avenue
Miami
Tel: 573-8042
This is a group of funky bars and clubs all under the one roof. It features some of the most unusual avant-garde Latin, Blues, Jazz and folk music acts in Miami.

Tobacco Road
626 South Miami Avenue
Tel: 374-1198
This is Miami's oldest bar and it is a great place to come and listen to live, late-night blues and jazz. It's crowded and smoky with excellent food, and the walls are covered in interesting memorabilia relating to the area. Open until 6am.

Zaragozona Lounge
8488 SW 8th Street
Tel: 267-5896
This is a classic Miami cocktail lounge where you can unwind with your favourite cocktail and enjoy the lively atmosphere.

Dancing/Discos

Churchill's
5501 NE 2nd Avenue, Miami
Tel: 757-1807
A hard-rock dance club with lots of ambience.

FAT/CATS POOL BAR
3390 Mary Street
Tel: 444-8081
Dance into the early hours at this wild entertainment complex.

LIQUID
1532 Washington Avenue
Miami Beach
Tel: 531-9411
Guarded by a velvet rope and muscle-bound body guards, this celebrity hang-out is one of the hottest dance clubs in the South Beach area.

CLUB MYSTIQUE
5101 Blue Lagoon Drive
(Airport Hilton Hotel)
Tel: 262-2780
A fun venue offering live Latin music and pulsating *salsa* dancing with lots of skin-tight pants and gyrating hips.

SHADOW LOUNGE
1532 Washington Avenue
Miami Beach
Tel: (305) 531-9411
Shadow Lounge attracts a fashionable, Euro-hip clientele with some of the world's top DJs.

Comedy Clubs

IMPROV COMEDY CLUB
3390 Mary Street
Tel: 441-8200
A dinner-club theater with local and national stand-up comics. Open Wednesday to Sunday.

RASCAL'S
8505 Mills Drive
Miami
Tel: (305) 274-5411

Cabaret

LES VIOLINS
1751 Biscayne Boulevard
Tel: 371-8668
Offers dinner-club stage-shows with plenty of fish-net stockings and brightly-colored feathers. Cultivates a flamboyant Latin flavor reminiscent of Havana's good old days. Open nightly except Monday.

CLUB TROPIGALA
4441 Collins Avenue
(Fontainebleau Hotel)
Miami Beach
Tel: 672-7469
Features live stage dancing, as well as music and magic shows Wednesday to Sunday.

COPACABANA
4410 W. 16th Avenue
Tel: 231-8898
Specialises in vivacious Cuban stage shows.

MALAGA
740 SW 8th Street
Little Havana
Tel: 858-4224
Dinner-club with Spanish singers and vibrating flamenco dancers. Closed Tuesday.

Calendar of Special Events

Orange Bowl Festival Miami's oldest festival, concerned with determining the country's college football champions. Celebrates with an evening parade on Biscayne Boulevard full of floats, feathers and beauty queens. Tel: 371-4600.

Art Deco Weekend (January) An Ocean Drive happening paying tribute to South Miami Beach's Art Deco architecture. Hotels are hard to find and the streets are filled with big-band sounds.

Coconut Grove Arts Festival (February) One of the largest arts festivals in the country, the Coconut Grove festival brings out the few remaining hippies in the area along with many slick, sophisticated artists. Tel: 539-3000.

Miami Film Festival (February) A week-long program of films shown at venues scattered throughout the city. The program fea-

tures a fine collection of foreign films from around the world produced during the year. Tel: 377-3456.

Miami Grand Prix (late February) A weekend of international car racing that gives the Monaco Grand Prix a run for its money. Tel: 539-3000.

MARCH/APRIL

Carnaval Miami/Calle Ocho Little Havana's 23-block long party of salsa, spicy foods and premeditated craziness. The purpose of the week-long festival is the celebration of Miami's Hispanic heritage and it includes music, drama and dance. The highlight is the final Sunday street party known as Calle Ocho which one year recorded the world's longest conga line as 119,986 people shimmied to the beat. Tel: 653-1877.

Italian Renaissance Festival (March) Vizcaya Museum and Gardens is the perfect setting for a col-

Goombay Festival

lection of mimes, concerts, and classical theater productions all done up in Italian Renaissance style.

MAY/JUNE

Coconut Grove Bed Race Wearing pajamas, and some rather skimpy ones at that, participants in the Grove Bed Race pile atop beds-on-wheels and charge down McFarlane Road.

Arabian Knights Festival (May) In the city of Opa-locka, an Arabian inspired architectural hodgepodge of minarets, domes and Ali Baba Avenue, the neighborhood's black community puts on a pageant of dress-up and make-believe honoring the city's history.

Miami/Bahamas Goombay Festival (June) Coconut Grove's Bahamian community welcomes the world to a weekend of Junkanoo madness, conch fritters and royal marching bands that stems from the historic celebration of the freeing of the slaves in the Bahamas. Tel: 539-3000.

JULY/AUGUST

Everglades Music and Crafts Festival Deep in the Florida Everglades west of the city, the native Florida Miccosukee Indian tribe puts on a

Calle Ocho in Little Havana

fair of alligator wrestling, air-boat rides, native crafts, music and foods.
Miami Reggae Festival (August) The entire Jamaican community turns out for this weekend party full of Rastaman vibrations in honor of Jamaica's Independence Day.

SEPTEMBER/OCTOBER

Columbus Day Regatta A Columbus Day weekend of sailing that starts at Coconut Grove's Dinner Key Marina, heads south to Elliot Key and back. Over 1,000 boaters take part and the emphasis is more on the spirit – and spotting topless bathers – than on the trophy.

OCTOBER/NOVEMBER

Miami Book Fair This week-long happening of book readings, autographing and lectures is a biblio-

Miami Grand Prix

phile's dream and proves to the world that Miami does have people who read. Tel: 237-3258.

NOVEMBER/DECEMBER

King Mango Strut (December) Miamians love festivals and the Mango Strut knows it. This silly Coconut Grove festival pokes fun at Miami – its politicians, famous people and problems.

Practical Information

By Air

The **Miami International Airport** is conveniently located right in the heart of the city, so travel time to most areas ranges from 10 minutes to Coral Gables to 25 minutes to Miami Beach. Over 85 scheduled carriers fly to Miami. Since it serves as the main hub to the Caribbean and Latin America,

the airport gets hectic and lines are often long for international flights. However, it is an easy terminal to get around because it is all contained in one structure.

Baggage claim areas for all airlines are located on the lower level. There is an airport hotel along with dozens of restaurants, banks, money exchange bureaux, bars, shops and lockers scattered throughout the concourses. For last minute tanning there's even a sun deck that overlooks the airfield at concourse E. The confirmation of flights – both domestic and international – is suggested. For general airport information Tel: 876-7000.

The **Fort Lauderdale International Airport** is about a 45-minute drive north of Miami airport and there are shuttle buses between the two.

By Rail

The passenger train network that travels across the US is **Amtrak** and it connects Miami with most major cities in the country. Rates are not as low as they are in other countries and a train pass from New York City to Miami will cost almost as much as a standard-fare airline ticket. But if you want to catch some scenery along the way, the trains are equipped with sleeping cabins and restaurant cars and the service on most provides for a good time.

A state transportation system called **Tri-Rail** links Miami daily on a varied

Rickenbacker Causeway

When to Visit

Naturally, Miami attracts more visitors in winter than in summer. Hotels have higher rates in 'season' – November to March – and the beach, attractions and restaurants get crowded. On the plus side, the weather is glorious and there are more entertainment choices. Spring and fall are quiet times and summer brings more families and travelers from South America.

schedule with the two northern counties of Broward and Palm Beach. Miami passengers can board the trains at the city's Metrorail station at 79th Street. For information Tel: 800-874-7245.

Travel Information

For general tourism information contact the Greater Miami Convention and Visitor's Bureau, 701 Brickell Avenue, Miami. Tel: 539-3000 or (toll free) 800-283-2707. Or try the Visit Florida website at www.flausa.com.

By Road

The roads are in excellent condition and driving is usually trouble free. However, a drive on the Florida state highway system tends to be rather boring because there is little to be viewed from the road and most of the state's topography is flat. Gas stations and restaurants dot the highways, as do far too many tacky tourist gift shops.

Speed limits range from 55–65mph, depending on the municipality. Normal city speed limits are 30mph; be aware that both limits are strictly enforced. The road journey between Miami and Orlando usually takes about 4 hours.

By Sea

If Miami happens to be one of your stops during a sail around the world, there are over 50 marinas in the area that cater to individual boaters and offer dock facilities and services for any size of craft. Cruise passengers who enter the **Port of Miami** – the largest cruise port in the world – are lucky because the port is just a 5-minute drive from downtown Miami and a trolley service is available. For general information about the port Tel: 371-7678.

Visas/Passports/Customs

As in all entry ports of the US, all foreign visitors must have a valid passport and some need visas and vaccination certificates depending on their country of origin. Canadian citizens usually don't need visas or passports. Agricultural products are forbidden, and because Miami is often used as an entry point for drug smuggling, the thorough checking of baggage at customs counters is common.

Climate

Miami's weather is its main draw to its millions of visitors. The average yearly temperature is a mild 75°F (24°C). November through March means warm days and breezy nights; sweaters and wind-breakers come in handy. April through October means hot days and mild nights; light clothing and pocket umbrellas are helpful. Protection from the sun is important to remember; many Miami vacations have been ruined by severe sun burn. Wide-brimmed hats and sunblock lotion are a necessity for those with fair skin.

Clothing

The city's reputation as a casual place holds true and shorts are always acceptable for men and women. Jackets with ties for men are only required in a few elegant restaurants and clubs. Bathing suits, although occasionally seen at the grocery stores, are only for the beach or pool.

Electricity

Standard electrical sockets operate on 110-volt current with 220-volt razor sockets available at most large hotels.

Time

Miami operates on Eastern Standard Time, which is Greenwich Mean Time minus 5 hours. From the last Sunday in April to the last Sunday in October, clocks are moved ahead one hour to observe Daylight Saving Time.

Helpful Information

Community organizations are abundant in Miami. Some of the helpful associations that offer assistance to travelers are:

Deaf Services Bureau 668-4407
Lighthouse for the Blind
 856-2288
Nursefinders
 418-4005
Babysitter Service
 923-9434
Alcoholics Anonymous
 371-7784
Gay and Lesbian Travel Association
 (954) 776-2626

GETTING ACQUAINTED

Population/Geography

Situated on the southeast coast of the US, Miami is closer to the Caribbean than to most major American cities, a factor which is evident in the landscape and the people. The greater Miami area sits within Dade County and is made up of 26 different municipalities each with its own local government offices. Tourism represents one of the area's main economic resources with about 7 million visitors annually. Other sources of income are international banking, agriculture, manufacturing and corporate headquarters.

Many of the area's 2 million residents come from Cuba or Latin America and about half the population speaks Spanish as their native language; the gregarious and warm Latin culture prevails. But if you listen carefully, you can also hear French Creole and Yiddish being spoken.

Christianity is the most commonly practiced religion. Judaism is abundant, and the Afro-Caribbean reli-

Dressed in Sunday best

gions of *santeria* and voodoo are also common. Houses of worship for most religions can be found in the city and are listed in the local telephone book.

Topographically, Miami is flat like the rest of the state. The average height above sea level is 10 feet. Hills only come in the form of bridges. The vegetation is lush and sub-tropical; bougainvillea, hibiscus and jasmine bloom year-round. Many backyards have mango, orange, grapefruit, and avocado trees. Exotic parrots, blown over from the Caribbean or escapees from area bird sanctuaries, are often heard and seen flying overhead.

Who Do You Trust?

Miami's status as a crime-ridden city is not undeserved. Although most travelers rarely encounter the crime problems which are often linked to illegal drug deals, there have been tragic exceptions. It's wise to use caution. Rental cars always indicate an easy target and robberies of passengers in their cars do happen. Remember to keep your car doors locked while in them and when parked, be careful with shoulder bags, and never leave luggage unattended. However, talking to strangers is still safe and don't let fear ruin a good local encounter.

Street corner life

Health and Emergencies

In case of accidents, crime, or emergencies, the toll-free telephone number to call is 911. This will connect you with both the local police and medical rescue units. Miami's medical facilities are excellent, but as there is no government-provided medicine all costs for any care have to be paid for by the individual. For dental referrals Tel: 667-3647. A 24-hour pharmacy can be found by calling Eckerd Drugs – 24-hour stores, Tel: 661-0778. For police non-emergencies Tel: 471-1780. For stolen or lost property Tel: 471-2900.

Money Matters

Major credit cards and traveler's checks are accepted at most establishments. Numerous banks and money exchange offices are available to change currencies along with a booth at Miami airport that is open 24 hours a day. Most banks are open from 9am–3pm Monday through Friday. Some are open on Saturday mornings. Cash machines can be found at most large shopping centers.

Gratuities are not added to most restaurant bills unless otherwise noted; the suggested rate is 15–20 percent of the total bill. The Florida state sales tax is 6 percent.

COMMUNICATION & MEDIA

Postal Service

Post offices in Dade County are open 8.30am–5pm Monday through Friday, and some are also open on Saturday from 8.30am–12 noon. For

general information on postal facilities Tel: 599-0166. All branches offer facilities including express mail, package deliveries and a holding service that allows out-of-towners to receive mail and parcels.

Telephones

Unless otherwise noted, all telephone numbers in this guide are preceded by the area code 305. All new telephone numbers installed in the Miami area after the summer of 1998 will require callers to dial (786) before dialing the regular number, but will still be considered a local call. If calling from another county or state dial (1) first. Telephone numbers preceded by "800" or "888" are charge-free within the US. For local telephone information Tel: 1-305-555-1212.

To dial other countries (Canada follows the US system), first dial the international access code 011, then the country code: **Australia** (61); **France** (33); **Germany** (49); **Italy** (39); **Japan** (81); **Mexico** (52); **Netherlands** (31); **New Zealand** (64); **South Africa** (27); **Spain** (34); **United Kingdom** (44). If using a US phone credit card, dial the company's access number below, then 01, then the country code. Sprint, Tel: 10333; AT&T, Tel: 10288.

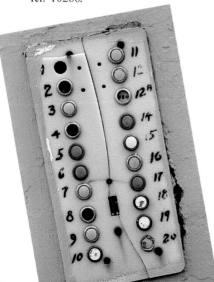

Media

South Florida's main newspaper is the *Miami Herald*. Along with good local and international news, it carries daily listings for area radio and television programs. The *Herald's* Friday edition includes a section on weekend events.

Area FM radio stations offer an assortment of music, and AM stations offer more news and talk programs.

Miami's alternative newspaper is the free weekly *New Times* which prints the most comprehensive listing of restaurants, arts and entertainment events available.

HOURS & HOLIDAYS

Businesses and shops are usually open Monday through Friday from 9am–5pm. Most large shopping areas are open from 10am–9.30pm Monday to Saturday and noon–6pm on Sunday.

During holidays, most government offices, businesses and banks are closed. Schools are also closed at these times so attractions and beaches are more congested. However, most restaurants are always open, even at Christmas.

January 1	New Year's Day
January 15	Martin Luther King's Birthday
February 12	Lincoln's Birthday
3rd Monday in February	Washington's Birthday
Last Monday in May	Memorial Day
July 4	Independence Day
1st Monday in September	Labor Day
2nd Monday in October	Columbus Day
November 11	Veterans Day
4th Thursday in November	Thanksgiving
December 25	Christmas

GETTING AROUND

Rental Cars

Miami is not an easy city to get around without a car and hitchhiking is illegal, but car rental rates in Florida are the lowest in the country.

Rental companies offer a range of autos from exotic sports cars to vans and economy models. Depending on time of year and the vehicle you want, fees vary from $80 to $600 per week.

Most major companies are located at the Miami airport and others are scattered throughout the city; they are all listed in the local telephone book. A few choices are:

Alamo Rent-a-car 633-6076
American Auto Rental 871-0494
Avis 668-3005
Budget 871-5331
Dollar 871-3926
Hertz 871-0300

Taxis

It's not easy to hail a cab in Miami; usually, a phone call is needed. But cabs are a convenient way to get around if you don't rent a car.

Taxis are always available at Miami airport and the fares to most destinations in the area cost between $15 and $20. All airport fares have one dollar added to the final bill. **General fares** are metered and rates are usually about $1.25 per mile no matter how many passengers are taken. The following are reliable companies:

Metro 888-8888
Best Yellow Taxi Service 445-4444
Society Cab 757-5523
Yellow 444-4444

In addition to taxis, SuperShuttle, a van service that transports passengers to and from the airport, is available 24 hours a day and can accommodate up to 11 people. Fares are lower than taxis. For information Tel: 871-2000.

Public Transit

Throughout Dade County there is a Metrobus system that connects with most parts of the city. The fare is $1 per person and the hours of operation vary with the route and day of the week. For maps or information about the system Tel: 770-3131.

Tour Companies

An easy first way to get acquainted with the city is to take one of the local tours. One of the more reputable tour operators in town is **Miami Nice Excursions**. Although based in Miami Beach, Miami Nice provides tourist pick-ups throughout the Miami area and offers a comprehensive tour of Miami and Miami Beach narrated by local guides. It also offers specially designed tours to meet specific interests. For information Tel: 931-8058.

The Miami Design Preservation League offers Saturday morning Art Deco walking tours conducted by area preservationists. They begin at 1224 Ocean Drive in Miami Beach. For information Tel: 672-1836.

Other tour companies include

Biscayne Helicopters (Tel: 252-3883) for helicopter tours of downtown, Tropical Balloons (Tel: 666-6645) for hot-air balloon tours of the Miami area, and the Historical Museum of Southern Florida (Tel: 375-1492) for historian-guided walking tours of many Miami neighborhoods.

ENTERTAINMENT

Tickets

For most events the main ticket sales office is Ticketmaster. For a small service charge, tickets can be purchased with credit cards by telephon-

ing 358-5885 and then picking it up at the venue. An area hot-line offers recorded information regarding current events, Tel: 372-1442.

Sports

For spectator sports in Miami there are several options. Football means the Miami Dolphins, Tel: 452-7000, or the University of Miami Hurricanes, Tel: 284-2655.

Miami's local basketball team is the Miami Heat and information on hometown games can be found by telephoning 530-4400.

Information on the Florida Marlins baseball team can be found by telephoning 626-7400.

Area soccer matches are held April to August Tel: 858-7477. Miami's West Indian community controls most of the Sunday cricket matches in the city, for locations Tel: 620-0275. Jai-Alai season runs November to September and the fast-paced game can be viewed at the Miami Jai-Alai fronton, Tel: 663-6400.

Racing comes in three forms. Thoroughbred horse racing is held at Calder Race Course Tel: 625-1311. Greyhound dog racing takes place at the Flagler Greyhound Track, Tel: 649-3000. Miami's Grand Prix auto racing monopolizes the city of Homestead once a year, usually in the end of February, for information Tel: 539-3000.

There are hundreds of tennis courts throughout the Miami area so it's a good idea to bring a racket. In addition to those located on the properties of major hotels, there are 25 public courts that usually charge an hourly fee. For locations call the Metro-Dade County Parks and Recreation Department, Tel: 579-2676.

Golf is also a favorite sport. Both 9 and 18-hole courses are open year round. Green fees range from $8 to $40 and reservations are suggested. For information about public courses Tel: 579-2968.

With 100 miles of flat, paved bike paths connecting the city, bicycling is popular. Dozens of rental shops are listed in the telephone directory. Since the streets are often congested with out-of-town drivers, helmets are a good idea and caution should be used at all times. For information call Dade County's Bicycle/Pedestrian Program Tel: 375-4507.

Biscayne Bay's calm waters make for good windsurfing and numerous

The Cavalier Hotel

rental businesses line the Ricken-backer Causeway on the way to Key Biscayne. A reliable choice for rentals and lessons is Sailboards Miami, Tel: 361-7245. Jet skis are also available in the same area, try Tony's Jet Ski Rentals Tel: 361-8280.

Fishing

Salt-water fishing takes place at bridges, piers and the surf throughout Miami. Boats for deep-sea fishing are available at Haulover Marina, Watson Island, MacArthur Causeway, Bayside Marketplace, and along Collins Avenue in Miami Beach.

WHERE TO STAY

It's not easy to find a bargain hotel in Miami and comparatively speaking they are quite expensive. In addition to the tourist trade in the city, Miami gets a large amount of American convention business which enables the hotels to charge higher rates. But during the off-season (April to October excluding summer), hotel rates are negotiable. Don't hesitate to ask for a lower rate than the one that is initially quoted, as hoteliers are often willing to strike a deal if there are empty rooms available.

The largest concentration of hotels is in Miami Beach. In South Miami Beach you will find Art Deco hotels which are small, charming and tropical. Toward the northern end of the beach are the larger grand-scale hotels. Coconut Grove and Coral Gables have a good selection of fine hotels to choose from.

All hotels in Miami have air-conditioning; 5 percent tax is placed on all hotel rooms in addition to the 6.5 percent sales tax. They also all accept most major credit cards such as American Express, Visa and Mastercard.

One exception to the expensive Miami hotel rule and a colorful anomaly is the **Miami Beach International Youth Hostel**. Located at 1438 Washington Avenue Tel: 800-379 2529 toll free, in the heart of the South Beach Art Deco District, the hostel is part of the international youth hosteling system. Dormitory rooms are comfortable and clean and reasonable around $17 per night. The historic Youth Hostel building is where Cuban band leader Desi Arnaz made his American debut in the 1950s.

The following categories are based on the lowest rates for a double room per night during the winter season. They are categorized as Expensive: above $250, Moderate: $150–250, and Inexpensive: under $150.

Expensive

ALEXANDER
5225 Collins Avenue, Miami Beach
Tel: 865-6500. Fax: 864-8525
An all-suite hotel for business travelers. Ocean and bay views, two heated pools, and a gourmet restaurant.

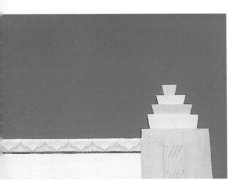

Detail from a Deco hotel

A waterfront hotel dotted with yachts and beautiful people. Tennis, golf, pool health club, and restaurants.

Moderate

MIAMI INTERNATIONAL AIRPORT HOTEL
Miami International Airport
Tel: 871-4100. Fax: 871-0800
This is the most convenient hotel for the airport.

HYATT REGENCY CORAL GABLES
50 Alhambra Plaza
Coral Gables.
Tel: 441-1234. Fax: 443-7702.
An urban high-rise that caters to business travelers and tourists. Mediterranean design, pool, health club.

HYATT REGENCY MIAMI
400 SE 2nd Avenue
Downtown
Tel: 358-1234. Fax: 358-0529.
A modern high-rise conveniently lo-

cated in the center of downtown Miami. Skyline and bay views, pool, good restaurants.

PLACE ST MICHEL
162 Alcazar Avenue,
Coral Gables.
Tel: 444-1666. Fax: 529-0074.
A small and historic hotel situated in the heart of the Gables. European antiques on the walls and in the corridors, as well as a gourmet-class restaurant.

FONTAINEBLEAU HILTON
4441 Collins Avenue
Miami Beach
Tel: 538-2000. Fax: 673-5351.
One of the luxury hotels that made Miami Beach famous in the 1950s. Over 1,000 refurbished rooms, many with views of the ocean, pool with waterfalls, good restaurants and a modern health spa.

GRAND BAY
2669 S Bayshore Drive
Coconut Grove
Tel: 858-9600. Fax: 859-2026
A plush, Mayan-style hotel overlooking the Dinner Key Marina and downtown skyline. Exquisite interior, pool, gourmet restaurant.

MAYFAIR HOUSE
3000 Florida Avenue
Coconut Grove
Tel: 441-0000 Fax: 446-0147.
A cleverly designed hotel in the heart of Coconut Grove. All rooms have hot tubs and many come equipped with pianos.

SONESTA BEACH RESORT
350 Ocean Drive
Key Biscayne
Tel: 361-2021. Fax: 361-3096
A casual beach resort decorated with Andy Warhol art. Pool, tennis, health club, restaurants.

TURNBERRY ISLE COUNTRY CLUB
19735 Turnberry Way
North Miami Beach
Tel: 932-6200. Fax: 937-0528.

Inexpensive

BAY HARBOR INN
9601 East Bay Harbor Drive
Bay Harbor
Tel: 868-4141. Fax: 868-4141
North of Miami Beach. Swimming pool, dock facilities and excellent restaurant.

CAVALIER
1225 Collins Avenue
Tel: 604-5064
Classic, small yet sophisticated Art Deco hotel a reasonable restaurant.

CARDOZO
1300 Ocean Drive
Miami Beach
Tel: 535-6500. Fax: 532-3563.
An Art Deco darling famous with the international modeling set. Ocean views and good service.

ESSEX HOUSE
1001 Collins Avenue
Miami Beach
Tel: 534-2700. Fax: 532-3827
Charming, characterful small Art Deco hotel.

EVERGLADES
244 Biscayne Boulevard
Downtown
Tel: 379-5461. Fax: 577-8445.
A reliable bet for many years, in the heart of Miami. Conveniently located for shopping. Swimming pool, restaurants.

BEST WESTERN MARINA PARK HOTEL
340 Biscayne Boulevard
Downtown
Tel: 371-4400. Fax: 372-2862
Within walking distance of Bayside Marketplace. French owned with tri-lingual service, swimming pool, restaurant.

MIAMI RIVER INN
118 SW South River Drive
Little Havana
Tel: 325-0045. Fax: 325-9227

An historic wooden inn in Little Havana overlooking the Miami river with antiques, old Florida charm, pool, jacuzzi.

FAIRFAX
1776 Collins Avenue
Miami Beach
Tel: 538-7082
Older, Deco-style hotel. Many rooms with kitchenettes and bargain rates. Parking can be a problem.

MARSEILLES
1741 Collins Avenue, Miami Beach
Tel: 538-5711
Another low-priced hotel that is clean and comfortable. Pool and some rooms with kitchenettes.

Campgrounds

Campsites for tents and hook-ups for recreational vehicles are available for travelers who like to bring their beds with them. All have showers, telephones, barbecuing and recreational facilities. The three most popular are the KOA North Miami, Tel: 940-4141; KOA South in a more rural area, Tel: 233-5300; and the Larry and Penny Thompson Park, Tel: 323-1049.

Index

Photography	**Tony Arruza** *and*
2/3, 8/9	**Bud Lee**
24	**Farrar, Straus & Giroux**
12T	**Historical Museum of Southern Florida/ Tony Arruza**
12B, 16	*Miami Herald*
Cover	**Randy Wells/Stone**
Back cover	**Glyn Genin**
Cover design	**Tanvir Virdee**
Cartography	**Berndtson & Berndtson**

Also from Insight Guides...

Insight Guides is the classic series, providing the complete picture with expert and informative text and stunning photography. Each book is an ideal travel planner, a reliable on-the-spot companion – and a superb visual souvenir of a trip. 193 titles.

Insight Maps are designed to complement the guidebooks. They provide full mapping of major destinations, and their laminated finish gives them ease of use and durability. 85 titles.

Insight Compact Guides are handy reference books, modestly priced yet comprehensive. The text, pictures and maps are all cross-referenced, making them ideal books to consult while seeing the sights. 119 titles.

INSIGHT POCKET GUIDE TITLES

Aegean Islands
Algarve
Alsace
Amsterdam
Athens
Atlanta
Bahamas
Baja Peninsula
Bali
Bali Bird Walks
Bangkok
Barbados
Barcelona
Bavaria
Beijing
Berlin
Bermuda
Bhutan
Boston
Brisbane & the
  Gold Coast
British Columbia
Brittany
Brussels
Budapest

California,
  Northern
Canton
Chiang Mai
Chicago
Corsica
Costa Blanca
Costa Brava
Costa Rica
Crete
Denmark
Fiji Islands
Florence
Florida
Florida Keys
French Riviera
  (Côte d'Azur)
Gran Canaria
Hawaii
Hong Kong
Hungary
Ibiza
Ireland
Ireland's
  Southwest

Israel
Istanbul
Jakarta
Jamaica
Kathmandu Bikes
  & Hikes
Kenya
Kuala Lumpur
Lisbon
Loire Valley
London
Los Angeles
Macau
Madrid
Malacca
Maldives
Mallorca
Malta
Manila
Marbella
Melbourne
Mexico City
Miami
Montreal
Morocco

Moscow
Munich
Nepal
New Delhi
New Orleans
New York City
New Zealand
Oslo and
  Bergen
Paris
Penang
Perth
Phuket
Prague
Provence
Puerto Rico
Quebec
Rhodes
Rome
Sabah
St. Petersburg
San Francisco
Sarawak
Sardinia
Scotland

Seville, Cordoba &
  Granada
Seychelles
Sicily
Sikkim
Singapore
Southeast England
Southern Spain
Sri Lanka
Sydney
Tenerife
Thailand
Tibet
Toronto
Tunisia
Turkish Coast
Tuscany
Venice
Vienna
Vietnam
Yogjakarta
Yucatán Peninsula